Praise for
Shape*Walking*

Bach worked with physical therapist and co-author, Schleck...on a program that takes simple walking to new heights of health...

    —Audrey DeLaMarte, Steps for Recovery, "Book and CD Reviews,"
    Sherman Oaks, California, February 1999

The anti-osteoporosis workouts were among the best I've come across in many books I've studied...It's a handsome book, well done...

    —Herman Mueller, Fifty Plus Fitness Association Bulletin,
    Stanford, California, Volume 3, 1998

Bach will help you make the most of your walking, adding strength and stretch for a well-rounded program that will enhance your life. Sound advice and clear, follow-along pictures ensure a safe, effective workout...

    —Junonia—catalog of active wear for women—Saint Paul, Minnesota,
    Fall 1998

The book has been written with beginners and seasoned athletes in mind... Along with this attention to detail, Marilyn L. Bach's Shape*Walking* will educate and encourage you to get into shape, have fun, and develop an overall healthier life.

    —Melpomene Institute, On the Move, Saint Paul, Minnesota,
    Summer 1998

Shape*Walking* is a well-thought-out, scientifically based, safe exercise program of moderate intensity. It meets the recommendations of the *1996 Surgeon General's Report on Physical Activity and Health.*

    —Arthur S. Leon, M.D., M.S., Taylor Professor and director of the
    Laboratory of Physiological Hygiene and Exercise Science, Division
    of Kinesiology, University of Minnesota

Exercise is an essential component of an effective psychiatric regimen. I highly recommend Shape *Walking* to private patients and busy corporate clients. It provides a thorough and effective approach to whole body health.
  —Alfred Messore, M.D., Washington, DC

Shape *Walking* fits into my busy personal and professional schedules. It works for me!
  —Janett Trubatch, Ph.D., vice chancellor for Research and Graduate Studies, University of Anchorage

My fifteen years experience with the mature adult fitness audience leads me to believe that Shape *Walking* is perfect for them!
  —Terri Wilcox, co-owner of Northern Athletics, Inc., Hudson, Wisconsin

I am hard-pressed to consistently take exercise classes or join an expensive health club. Shape *Walking* provides a fitness program that I can do at home or when I travel.
  —Barbara Laska, national franchise business manager, Tosco Marketing Company, Phoenix, Arizona

Since the band fits perfectly into my flight bag, I can maintain my exercise schedule during hectic business trips.
  —Joyce Schmidt, president and CEO of Creative Connections, New London, Connecticut

Shape *Walking* is a great program for senior citizens. I feel more flexible and strong after only six weeks. I am so thrilled with Shape *Walking* that I convinced my sister to join the next session.
  —Betty Kachel, Woodbury, Minnesota

Shape*Walking*
Six Easy Steps to a Healthier Life

heelto **toe**
FITNESS WALKING, INC.®

Shape*Walking*

Six Easy Steps to a Healthier Life

Marilyn L. Bach, Ph.D.
with Lorie Schleck, M.A., P.T.

A Publication of

In Your Best Interest

The advice presented in this guide is not a substitute for medical counseling. If you have a history of any medical problems, particularly heart and/or respiratory conditions, lower limb and/or feet problems, and/or osteoporosis, you *must* see your doctor before beginning any fitness program. Even if you have vague concerns about your health or you haven't had a physical for a few years, consult a licensed physician before increasing physical activity.

Publisher's Cataloging-in-Publication Data
(Provided by Quality Books, Inc.)

Bach, Marilyn L.
    Shapewalking : six easy steps to a healthier life / Marilyn L. Bach with Lorie Schleck. – 1st ed.
    p. cm.
    Includes bibliographical references.
    LCCN: 98-65831
    ISBN: 0-9662975-0-4

    1. Walking. 2. Physical fitness. 3. Exercise.
I. Schleck, Lorie. II. Title

RA781.65.B33 1998   613.7'176
               QBI99-283

In memory of my mother, Ida, whose regimen of daily walks and indomitable will inspired its writing.

Marilyn L. Bach, Ph.D.

Preface

I am often asked, "What led you to develop the *ShapeWalking* program?" My answer has two parts: The first is profoundly personal; the second is based on scientific studies.

The most personal answer to this question is that, above all, I am alive today! A life-threatening medical complication occurred in late 1995 as a result of routine surgery. Most of 1996 was spent in and out of hospitals, to be seen by multiple specialists—who were stunned that I was in fact still here—attributing my survival to a lifelong commitment to exercise.

As I returned to health, I attended a fitness walking workshop led by internationally ranked racewalker Sage Cowles. A pivotal high-point, this workshop clarified the way I could bring my commitment to exercise to the general public. I became a personal trainer specializing in fitness walking—an exercise much of the general public can do. Continuing to recuperate, I "landed" on Lorie Schleck's physical therapy table. We soon discovered a mutual interest in the essential role of exercise for health. A new collaboration began between Lorie's expertise and mine. During our physical therapy sessions, *ShapeWalking* was born!

We determined only a three-part program containing heart-healthy exercise, resistance-strength training, and stretching would give people the *full package* needed for complete health and fitness. We designed *ShapeWalking* to be portable, accessible, and affordable. We offer it now to you—and hope you take six easy steps to a healthier life.

Marilyn L. Bach, Ph.D.
January 1998

Acknowledgments

The authors wish to thank the following individuals for technical advice: Terri Wilcox, *Northern Athletics, Inc.,* Hudson, Wisconsin; Shawn O'Brien, *Fitness on the Move,* Sebastopol, California; Sage Cowles and Sandra Viele, *The Sweatshop,* Saint Paul, Minnesota; Jane Norstrom, M.A., *HealthSystem Minnesota;* Robert Serfass, Ph.D., and Arthur Leon, M.D., Division of Kinesiology, *University of Minnesota.*

A special thanks to clients who gave their input: Darlene Kvist, Barbara Brenner, Rondi Nervig, and Kay Fitchett. The authors wish to particularly acknowledge the coordinators and clients of the Saint Paul Community Education System for supporting a pilot program of Shape *Walking* through workshops and classes.

Special acknowledgments to: Susan Stuart Otto, Tom Oberg, Jack Caravela, Kate Bandos, Don Korbin, and Kris Diemer for guidance; Genny Freier, Gail Helland, Chris Roerden, Sandy Delos, and Connie Anderson for editing; Carol Nies, Xan R. Guzik, Anna I. Esser, Leslie Walters, and Judith Zubick for editorial assistance.

Photography and initial graphic design by Anna I. Esser, Saint Paul, Minnesota. Book design by Karla K. Caspari with design assistance from Ryan Walton and production assistance from Shar Jessie and Michelle McCoy, *Caspari Design Group,* Minneapolis, Minnesota. Fitness wardrobe is courtesy of *Run N Fun,* Saint Paul, Minnesota.

About the Authors

Marilyn L. Bach, Ph.D.

Marilyn L. Bach, Ph.D., is the founder and owner of *Heel to Toe Fitness Walking*, Saint Paul, Minnesota, and designer of the Shape *Walking* program. Dr. Bach is a personal trainer certified by the American Council on Exercise and a member of the American College of Sports Medicine. She has extensive experience as a research scientist/faculty member at several graduate and medical schools, including the Massachusetts Institute of Technology, the University of Wisconsin School of Medicine, and the University of Minnesota Medical School.

Lorie Schleck, M.A., P.T.

Lorie Schleck, M.A., P.T., is a physical therapist with more than thirteen years' experience in sports medicine. She is currently coordinator for the Institute for Athletic Medicine's Running Program at Fairview Hospital, Minneapolis, Minnesota. Ms. Schleck specializes in treating injuries in active individuals and advising them about sports and fitness training. Simultaneously, she maintains a high national profile by serving as a continuing education instructor to physical therapists, with a particular emphasis on bio-mechanics of the lower extremities. To ensure that she is at the cutting edge of functional knowledge of the musculoskeletal system, Ms. Schleck participates in advanced training courses at both the local and national levels.

Contents

Making the Decision— Is Shape*Walking* for You?

Why Is Shape*Walking* Right for Your Health and Overall Fitness?

Welcome to Shape*Walking!* This easy, low-cost program has been designed for you as a total fitness package. A total fitness program includes aerobic/heart-healthy exercise, strength training, and stretching.

Shape*Walking* starts with fitness walking, a variation of ordinary walking, and then adds simple techniques to improve muscle strength and flexibility. Unlike other strength training fitness programs, Shape*Walking* doesn't require the use of heavy weights, so there is no need to join an expensive health club or purchase costly home equipment. Shape*Walking*'s use of bands is very different from any other "band" workout on the market. To avoid latex allergies common to our population, Shape*Walking* uses a non-latex band. Shape*Walking*'s strength exercises never require "anchor points" for your band. Your body provides all the anchoring you need. Shape*Walking* provides flexibility stretching exercises for your body's major muscle groups that increase your range of motion and prevent injury. The three components—fitness walking, resistance-strength training, and safe flexibility stretching—make Shape*Walking* a flexible and portable total fitness program.

The following pyramid graphically depicts the three-part Shape*Walking* program, a complete fitness package.

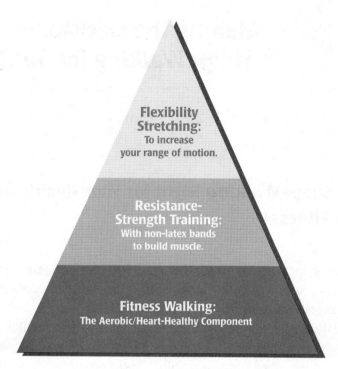

Shape *Walking: A Total Fitness Program*

Shape *Walking* is an extremely versatile program that can be done by anyone, anywhere, anytime. Whether you are an experienced exerciser or someone working out for the very first time—whether you are old or young, physically fit or a couch potato—Shape *Walking* can help improve your overall level of fitness and health. This book guides you to Shape *Walking* in six easy steps. The Shape *Walking* Photo Shoot presents your program choices in easy-to-follow photos.

Step 1 begins by defining "fitness" and showing how the Shape *Walking* program contains all the major components of the fitness concept. You will learn the difference between ordinary walking and fitness walking and how fitness walking, combined with other components of the Shape *Walking* program, can benefit your health.

What Does Fitness Mean to You?

What do you think about when you think about getting fit? Will it be too hard? Does it mean being thinner? Stronger? Feeling better emotionally? Having more energy? Being able to spring back after a hard day at home or work? These are some of the things people commonly think about when they hear the word *fitness.*

Shape*Walking* defines fitness as the effective integration of mind and body through exercise. Mentally, you may experience reduced stress and a higher sense of self-esteem and accomplishment. Physically, you will improve in the five major areas of fitness: cardiovascular and respiratory health, muscular strength, endurance, flexibility, and body tone. Improving your fitness level physically and mentally will put more bounce in your step, give you more energy, and yes, you will feel fit!

Experts tell us that to get our health and fitness benefits, the most effective exercises involve dynamic, rhythmic movements of major muscle groups. Fitness walking, the heart-healthy component of Shape*Walking*, accomplishes this exercise goal and is easy, safe, and inexpensive. When the additional benefits of strength training and flexibility stretching are added, Shape*Walking* techniques give you have a total fitness package!

Walking Is Good for Your Health!

The Surgeon General, blue ribbon panels from the National Institutes of Health, and many professional health media sources stress that regular physical activity is vital to your health and well-being. And the *1996 Surgeon General's Report on Physical Activity and Health* specifically recommends walking, especially brisk walking (fitness walking), for all ages. Walking can add years and quality to your life.

Walking Is Easily Accessible...and Low Risk

Millions of Americans can easily include walking in their fitness programs because walking requires only two things: properly fitting athletic shoes and somewhere to walk—a scenic path, or perhaps a shopping mall, indoor track, or treadmill for bad weather. And fitness walking is extremely low risk. With runners and joggers suffering a host of overuse injuries (including painful shin splints), many fitness and athletic trainers believe the late 1990s will spark an era of walking, especially fitness walking. The impact of jogging or running on your lower limbs is approximately three times your body weight, while the impact of fitness walking is only about 1.3 times your body weight. It's easy to see why fitness experts applaud walking's low injury risk.

> **The impact of jogging or running on your lower limbs is approximately three times your body weight, while the impact of fitness walking is only about 1.3 times your body weight. It's easy to see why fitness experts applaud walking's low injury risk.**

Fitness Walking and Weight Loss

For many individuals, losing weight and maintaining weight loss are important goals. The sedentary lifestyle fostered by modern technology has exacerbated weight control for many Americans.

Using fitness walking as your primary heart-healthy exercise can help with weight loss, too. Your Shape*Walking* program will help you lose weight and maintain your weight loss.

Adding resistance-strength training to your walking program will help you build and maintain muscles that burn up more calories than fat! So be sure to include two or three sessions of resistance training per week. The Shape*Walking* program is *designed* to work your body's major muscle groups. If you don't see a major change on your scale, don't be alarmed. Remember that muscle weighs more than fat! As you build and strengthen your body's major muscle groups, you may even gain pounds, but you will notice a difference in how you feel and look—strong, svelte, and energized!

As a lifetime approach to weight control and healthy living, increase your activity level during your daily routine. Hide your TV remote control. Take the stairs instead of the elevator. Park your car several blocks from your destination. Add steps to your day...Just get movin'!

Fitness Walking Is Different from Everyday Walking

When fitness professionals talk about walking, they generally mean fitness walking—an exercise that almost anybody can do with proper training because it's so easy. Fitness walking differs from ordinary walking. Fitness walking:

◆ Has a *form*. It emphasizes proper posture, alignment, and technique as critical elements to achieving goals.

◆ Sets a faster pace—from 13 to 18 minutes per mile.

◆ Keeps your heart rate in the "target zone." In fact, keeping your heart rate at target is the key element of fitness walking.

Every time you find a chance to "slip into high gear" by changing from ordinary walking to fitness walking, you are working toward a healthy heart. Plus, you quickly burn more calories. And the best part is the low cost, because all you really need are comfortable clothes and a pair of good shoes!

The Benefits of Fitness Walking

Fitness walking:

◆ Promotes and maintains weight loss.

◆ Promotes self-confidence.

◆ Boosts mood and energy.

◆ Improves flexibility.

◆ Helps manage stress, anxiety, depression.

◆ Has a low risk of injury.

◆ Promotes cardiovascular health.

◆ Is a life-long activity.

◆ Reduces risk of osteoporosis.

◆ Promotes ideal posture.

These benefits can help you live longer and be healthier. Best of all, fitness walking is fun!

What Does Strength Mean to You?

Does the phrase *strength training* make you think of Arnold Schwarzenegger and bulging biceps? Competitive body-building for titles is certainly one kind of strength training where you imagine Mr. Universe lifting an extremely heavy weight a single time. But there are many different ways to build muscle mass and strength, and not all of them are so extreme.

Remember that Shape*Walking* defines fitness as the effective integration of mind and body through exercise. An essential part of fitness is strength building. Medical studies show that strength is critical to health and well-being. When you hear the words *strength training*, you need to think about the "overload principle." The overload principle means building muscle mass and strength by challenging the muscle multiple times with progressively heavier weight or resistance. As Wayne L. Westcott, Ph.D., nationally recognized authority on fitness training, states, "Strength training is the process of exercising with progressively heavier resistance for the purpose of strengthening the musculoskeletal system." Building muscle mass does not necessarily mean building muscle bulge. Repeating this process many times during an exercise session is an effective muscle builder.

There is good news and bad news about muscle strength. The bad news is that you can lose it—partly from normal aging but especially from lack of use. When muscle strength is lost, your ability to perform even routine daily tasks suffers. Have you ever known someone who became bed ridden after an accident or because of a long illness? After a while, these people became weak, maybe even frail without necessary exercise.

The good news is that muscle strength needn't be lost through disuse or normal aging. And it can even be increased...*no matter at what age you start your fitness program.*

Fitness walking alone is not enough to maintain your strength. You need strength training, too. When strength training and flexibility training are added to heart-healthy walking, you have the means to reach all your fitness goals.

Benefits of Resistance-Strength Training

Like fitness walking, the benefits of strength training are also enormous. One important benefit is an increase in metabolic rate. Metabolic rate refers to the total amount of calories your body burns over a 24-hour period to keep your body at a constant temperature and functioning normally, not including extra energy needed for exercise. Unlike fat, which stores calories, muscle burns calories. This is where strength training can help with weight loss and control. Muscles burn calories even when you are not exercising. Muscles need energy for normal cell maintenance and to generate body heat. The greater the muscle mass in your body, the more calories you burn automatically throughout the day and at night. Research has shown that non-training adults can experience as much as a 0.5 percent reduction in metabolic rate per year—a loss that strength training can help prevent.

Strength training:

◆ Improves the ability to function in daily life.

◆ Combats frailty in the elderly.

◆ Reduces risk of injury.

◆ Improves physical appearance.

◆ Improves self-confidence.

Strength Training Fights Osteoporosis

Strength training can be effective in both preventing and fighting osteoporosis (overly porous bones). Strength training increases both bone density and bone strength. Improving bone density and bone strength are key factors in preventing or even reversing osteoporosis. In studies where osteoporosis patients used strength training on major muscle groups, including common osteoporosis sites, bone density loss was actually reversed.

Some fitness trainers define strength training as the ability to lift a heavy weight one time. But Shape*Walking* is a program that doesn't require heavy weights, health club memberships, or expensive home equipment. So how does Shape*Walking* increase strength?

The answer is: progressive resistance training!

The resistance-strength training element of Shape *Walking* applies the same principle that physical therapists use to rehabilitate their patients. Rather than lifting a heavy weight, the Shape *Walker* uses her own body weight and/or pulls against the resistance of a non-latex Shape *Walking* band. The program uses four bands, in different colors, of progressively higher resistance.

What Does Flexibility Mean to You?

Flexibility is defined as "the range of motion around a joint." Inactivity, injury, or certain disease states tend to decrease flexibility, potentially compromising your ability to perform daily tasks of life. *Functional* flexibility is attained when individuals have a range of motion that allows them to go about their normal activities of daily living without restrictions.

Functional flexibility differs for each individual. The injured gymnast may wish to resume an athletic program that requires an extraordinary degree of flexibility—that extraordinary degree of flexibility is functional for her. In sharp contrast, the goal of an individual with osteoarthritis may be to perform daily activities such as walking, cooking, and shopping, or to function in a profession that may require conducting meetings, presentations at seminars, etc. Functional flexibility differs significantly for each of these two individuals.

Benefits of Flexibility Stretching

Flexibility stretching:
◆ Promotes a sense of well-being.
◆ Relaxes the mind and body.
◆ Reduces stiffness.

- Reduces muscle tension and soreness.
- Promotes improved coordination.
- Allows for freer movement.
- Prevents injuries such as muscle strains.
- Increases range of motion.
- Develops body awareness.
- Promotes improved circulation.
- Is peaceful and non-competitive.
- Prepares the body for movement.
- Promotes improved posture and balance.
- Improves the body's ability to withstand stress or strain.

Fitness Walking + Resistance-Strength Training + Flexibility Stretching = Shape*Walking*

So now you have met with the three basic elements that make Shape*Walking* a total fitness package. Your complete Shape*Walking* routine will consist of:

- A warm-up.
- Fitness walking.
- A Shape*Walking* resistance-strength training program.
- A cool-down.
- Flexibility stretching.

From the Shape*Walking* Photo Shoot, you will be able to choose one of three tailor-made strength and stretching workouts that fits your goals and schedule. Integral to each workout are fitness walking—the five-day-a-week, heart-healthy workout—and Mat Workout, which targets abdominal and back muscles. The Mat Workout requires a comfortable, flat surface, like a floor, and is probably best done at home. The Mat Workout should be done in conjunction with any tailor-made workout you choose and should be done at least two days a week with a rest day in between.

The three tailor-made strength and stretching programs are:

◆ The **20-Minute Workout**—a short yet effective routine...

◆ The **Anti-Osteoporosis Workout**—the 20-minute workout plus exercises selected specifically to combat osteoporosis. *Great for women approaching their fourth decade and beyond.*

◆ The **Comprehensive Workout**—an extensive and complete routine...

Never let boredom keep you from participating in your Shape*Walking* program. Have fun!

Getting Started with Fitness Walking

You have decided to learn Shape *Walking*! Congratulations! Step 2 tells you everything you need to get started with fitness walking.

Getting Started Is EASY!

Some tips to help you get movin'!

◆ Start a fitness walking program by participating in a fitness walking workshop or by taking lessons from an experienced instructor certified by a credible national organization, such as the American Council on Exercise or the American College of Sports Medicine.

◆ Find a friend who will accompany you on your fitness walks.

◆ Join a local fitness walking group.

◆ Make walking an everyday habit like brushing your teeth or combing your hair.

◆ Schedule walks into your day.

◆ Set both short- and long-term goals.

◆ Reward yourself for reaching a short-term goal.

◆ Treat yourself to a massage, a new walking shirt, a facial, or a manicure as a reward for starting.

◆ Be your own coach and cheerleading squad.

- Pace yourself.
- Above all else...have fun!

> **For bad weather days, a treadmill is a terrific choice for indoor exercise. Fitness walking on a treadmill uses the same muscles as fitness walking in a mall or park— the technical differences are insignificant. Use the same six-step plan presented in this manual. Remember to stretch at the end of your treadmill workout!**

Wear the Right Shoes, Comfortable Clothes ... and a Smile!

Having appropriately designed and properly fitting athletic shoes is essential

- Purchase athletic shoes from a reputable business that specializes in athletic footwear. (If you wear orthotics, be sure to take them with you when you purchase your walking shoes.)
- Look for a walking shoe with a cushioned, flexible sole and a top/upper that lets the foot *breathe* or allows air to circulate around the foot and moisture to escape. Avoid plastic or rubber walking shoes.
- Look for a high and wide toe box.
- Look for a *wedge* heel. It helps the foot rock from heel to toe. Since fitness walking is a lower impact sport than running, the heel of a walking shoe does not need to be as high or broad as that of a running shoe.
- Be sure the shoe has good traction and is capable of absorbing shock.

◆ Be sure to try on shoes in the store. Wear the socks you will walk in, and walk around a while before you decide.

Some shoe options presently on the market: Asics™ GT 2030, Adidas™ Solo-W, Nike™ Walk/Run, and the Ryka™ Flexor.

Choosing appropriate socks is also important

◆ Purchase walking socks from a reputable dealer that specializes in athletic footwear. If you are not sure what to get, let a knowledgeable salesperson help you select a pair right for the environmental conditions you are usually walking in—inside a gym or outside during a wicked winter's day.

◆ Wear athletic socks that are adequately cushioned and have effective "wicking" properties. In other words, they draw the perspiration away from your foot.

Now that you're outfitted in proper foot gear, let's turn to the rest of your outfit.

Choosing appropriate clothing for walking depends on the weather

◆ Dress in layers suitable to the weather so you can add or remove clothing if the weather changes during your workout or as your body temperature changes with the intensity of your workout.

◆ Body clothing that wicks moisture away from your body is preferred by some walkers, but it's not as important as having wicking fabric in your socks.

◆ Reflective clothing is always a good idea, even in the daytime.

Don't let extreme weather conditions deter your workout. If you choose to walk outdoors during extreme weather, you need to consider your clothing very carefully.

Exercising in hot weather

◆ Avoid restrictive clothing or materials that prevent evaporation of sweat, such as nylon. Fishnet or loose cotton clothing is suggested. Dress in layers so that you can remove outer clothing as you approach your target zone.

◆ Wear a cap with a visor to protect your head and partially shade your eyes. Sunglasses will cut the sun's glare and reduce the strain on your eyes.

◆ Take special precautions when it's hot and humid. Drink plenty of water; cut your exercise session when you become uncomfortable. Do *not* drink alcohol before or during your exercise session. It will dehydrate you!

Exercising in cold weather

◆ Wear a cap, scarf, and gloves, preferably "thermal." A waterproof shell and pants, preferably of "breathable" material, are recommended.

◆ Choose clothing carefully. Dress in layers so that your clothing traps air for increased warmth. It's best to dress in **three** layers:

• The Wicking Layer—inner

Wear non-absorbent materials like polyester, olefin, synthetic polyester, polypropylene, thermax for socks, hats, and underwear.

• The Insulation Layer—middle

Wear fabrics such as Thinsulate™, Polar Plus™, and Polar Fleece™ for jacket liners and pullovers.

• The Protective Layer—outer

Wear water-repellent, breathable fabrics like Versatech™ and Gamex™ for light exercise. For extreme weather conditions, wear high-tech laminates that are waterproof with moderate breathability like Gore-Tex™ and Thintech™.

- Wear your hat! Studies have shown that 20 to 60 percent of heat is lost through an uncovered head. Find a cheerful, colorful one with a tassel, or whatever fits your fancy!
- Wear sunglasses to filter out harmful ultraviolet rays. Yes, even in the winter!
- Take special care to protect the nose, chin, and fingers, as they tend to get colder than other areas.
- Wear shoes with adequate grip. For particularly slippery surfaces, shoe chains are available in running stores.

A major advantage of fitness walking is its low cost; however, properly fitting shoes are most important. So if you are budgeting, put your money into good shoes and socks. Your clothing can be just about anything loose and comfortable that allows you to move easily.

What Is the Target Zone?

Do you remember the key difference between everyday walking and fitness walking?

**Keeping your heart rate in the target zone
is the key to fitness walking.**

What exactly do fitness professionals mean when they talk about the target zone? How can you find out what your target zone is?

Adequate intensity achieves results

To reap the harvest of health and fitness benefits, you need to walk with the right amount of intensity. That means warming up and walking quickly enough to reach a heart rate of 65 percent to 85 percent of your maximum heart rate (the target zone) and to keep walking at that rate until it's time for your cool-down. Walking too slowly is not as beneficial as walking with adequate intensity. Walking too fast can increase the chance of injury. So, how do you know if you are walking at the correct speed?

Target Zone: 65% to 85% of your Maximum Heart Rate

There are three ways to make sure you are walking in your target zone: the talk test, perceived exertion, and monitoring your pulse rate.

Target zone: the talk test

This is the fastest and easiest way to check your effort. Just ask yourself, "Could I carry on a conversation with a friend walking beside me, right now?" If you answer, "No, I'm out of breath. It would be difficult or impossible to carry on a conversation right now." *Slow down* immediately!

If you answer, "Yes, I could easily carry on a conversation right now. In fact, I think I could work a little harder!" Try to speed up and increase your effort just a bit. Keep giving yourself the talk test, and as soon as you think you couldn't "walk the walk *and* talk the talk," *slow down!*

Target zone: perceived exertion

Picture a scale from 0 to 10. Zero is the feeling you have when you are not exerting at all, and 10 is the feeling you have with extreme exertion. Now rate yourself from 0 to 10. **Level 5 to Level 7** is the **TARGET ZONE**.

How do you think you feel?

PERCEIVED EXERTION SCALE

0 _____ **5 to 7**_____ 10

TARGET ZONE

Level

0 = No exertion—same feeling you have when simply awake and relaxed

1 = Very slight exertion—very weak

2 = Slightly more exertion, but still weak

3 = Light to moderate exertion

4 = Moderate exertion

5 = Moderate to strong exertion—same feeling you have when walking **deliberately** as if on your way to an appointment

6 = Strong exertion—same feeling you have when walking as if you are **5 minutes late** for an appointment

7 = Stronger exertion—same feeling you have when walking as if you are **10 minutes late** for an appointment

8 = Increased exertion over **Level 7**—definitely exerting but you can finish your walking routine

9 = Very strong exertion, increased exertion over **Level 8**—you can't talk and continue walking. You should *not* be experiencing a **Level 9** on a routine basis and should *slow down or quit for the session* if you feel you are working at a **Level 9.**

10 = Extreme exertion—same feeling you have with all-out physical activity. You should never experience a **Level 10.**

On the perceived exertion scale, depending on your goal, you will eventually be exercising between **Levels 4 and 8.** Exercising between **Levels 5 and 7,** the target zone, is sufficient to achieve the goals of most people, without risk of over-training/overuse injuries. Only highly conditioned, elite athletes train at **Levels 9 and 10.**

Target zone: taking your pulse

This method is a little more complicated than the talk test or perceived exertion, because you will actually take your pulse and get a number of beats per minute rather than simply relying on how you feel.

To determine your heart rate, take your pulse for 10 seconds in the middle of your exercise routine. Then multiply that figure by 6. For example, suppose you took a ten-second pulse and got 20. Multiplying 20 times 6 is 120 beats per minute. Good enough, but now what? Compare your number to your maximum heart rate (MHR).

**Maximum Heart Rate (MHR) equals
the number 220 minus your age**

For example:

A target zone needs a low end (minimum) and a high end (maximum). The low end is defined as 65 percent of the MHR and the high end is 85 percent of the MHR.

Using this rule of thumb, a 50-year-old walker's MHR would be $220-50 = 170$.

**Low End = .65 X MHR = .65 X 170 = 111 beats per minute.
High End = .85 X MHR = .85 X 170 = 145 beats per minute.
Target Zone = 111 to 145 beats per minute.**

In our example, the walker needs to walk so that her heart rate is more than 111 beats per minute but less than 145 beats per minute. Since the exercise pulse rate (see above) was 120 beats per minute, she is walking within target zone.

For those of you interested in keeping a continuous check on your heart rate, wear a commercially available heart rate monitor during your entire exercise session.

How Long Should You Walk at the Target Zone?

Now that you know what your individual target zone is, how many minutes should you walk at target zone during your exercise outing? Knowing *your* baseline is important. Here's a simple method.

Choose a safe, well-lit, and familiar route of known or measured distance that you can comfortably walk. For example, walk around a block near your home. Dress comfortably and wear appropriate walking shoes.

First, warm up by walking at your usual walking pace for five to seven minutes. After you have warmed up, note what time it is. This is the beginning of your exercise period. You are now starting to walk in your target zone.

Now, walk at a brisk, steady pace (strong exertion) as if you are on your way to an appointment. If you are feeling more vigorous, walk **as if you are five minutes late** for your appointment, which will increase intensity. Keep at this pace until you feel uncomfortable or breathless.

As soon as you feel uncomfortable or breathless, *slow down* and make note of the time. This is the *end* of your exercise period. Allow yourself to cool down by walking slowly for five to seven minutes.

Subtract the number of minutes from the beginning of your exercise period to the end. This is the amount of time you were able to walk comfortably in your target zone. It's your own starting baseline.

Warm-up _____ **STARTING BASELINE** _____ **Cool-down**
5 to 7 minutes   Begin – walk at Target Zone – End*   5 to 7 minutes

*End equals you can't talk/breathless.

Remember that the most important thing is simply to get movin'. It's fine, in fact highly desirable, to do what's comfortable for your body. So feel free just to walk normally during your outings!

Find a friend who will accompany you on your fitness walks.

Wear the right shoes, comfortable clothes...and a smile!

Above all else...have fun!

Now You're Movin'!

OK! Shoes on. Warmed up. Let's take a fitness walk!

Proper Fitness Walking Technique

For proper posture

◆ Stand tall with head held high.

◆ Hold body erect, head up. Keep eyes looking ahead. Keep chin straight, parallel to the ground, and not jutting forward.

◆ Draw an imaginary straight line connecting ear, shoulder, hip, knee, and ankle down each side of the body.

◆ Do not bend at the waist or slouch at the shoulder. Check your posture in a mirror or the reflective glass in a store window as you walk past.

Arm movement and position are important

Casey Meyers, a national authority on fitness walking technique, describes well the proper arm movement in his book, *Walking:*

◆ Hold your hands in loose, closed fists, with your thumbs resting on top of your fingers.

- Bend your arms 90 degrees at the elbow.

- Pump your bent arms vigorously back and forth, but naturally. Do not cross the front midline of your body.

- Swing your arms forward, no higher than your breast while holding your arms close to the body.

- Swing your arms back so that your closed fists meet the side seam of your pants.

- Keep your shoulders relaxed and square.

Leg movement and position propel you

- Your legs should swing forward naturally with your knee almost fully extended.

Foot placement is very important

- Land with a heel strike with the foot of your leading leg.

- Strike with the heel; allow the foot to roll from heel to toe.

- Push off from the ball of your trailing foot (*toe-off*). The foot placement path should form two straight, narrow parallel lines.

Hip motion is a natural movement

- Allow your pelvis to have a natural forward and backward motion.

- Do not swing hips from side to side.

- Keep your hips relaxed.

Breathing correctly helps endurance

- Breathe deeply down into your abdomen.

- Allow the air to completely fill your lungs.

- Avoid shallow breathing or panting.

- Exhale, flattening your tummy.

Technique for increased speed

◆ Pump your bent arms vigorously.

◆ Shorten stride length–take short, quick steps.

Walk Tall

1. Head erect, eyes forward, chin parallel to ground.

2. Hand in loose fist.

3. Heel strike.

4. Toe push.

5. Elbow back, bent 90 degrees.

6. Shoulders square.

Fitness walking at the Capitol, Saint Paul, Minnesota.

Be Alert to Your Needs and Surroundings

Safety

◆ Carry ID and enough money for a phone call. Vary your route and stay alert to your surroundings. If you wear a headset, don't have it so loud that you can't hear oncoming cars. Wear reflective clothing for evening walks. Leave hand weights at home! They will put you at risk for forearm and shoulder injuries and can increase your blood pressure.

Hydration

◆ Whatever the weather, be sure to drink water before, during, and after your workout. (See page 44 for details.) There are some very comfortable waist packs designed to carry a water bottle as well as your identification and that important pocket change.

Skin

◆ Wear sunscreen with a sun protection factor of 15 or higher. Yes, even in the winter! Cold weather actually heightens the skin's sun susceptibility.

◆ On cold, windy days, walk against the wind at first and return with the wind at your back. This way, perspiration will not cool on your skin and chill your body.

Posture

◆ Check body's alignment in a mirror or the reflective glass of a store window.

Breathing

◆ Inhale deeply; exhale slowly.

Warm-up

◆ Simply walking at your regular pace for five to seven minutes is a good warm-up.

◆ In hot weather, begin your warm-up slowly to allow your body to adjust to the heat.

Target zone exercise

◆ Start with your own individual baseline (amount of time you can comfortably walk in your target zone).

◆ Keep adding time and gradually progress to your individual goals.

Cool-down

◆ A minimum of five minutes followed by a flexibility stretching period.

Setting Realistic and Attainable Goals

For most people, achieving overall health, fitness, or weight control is the goal.

If your goal is overall health

Recent studies have shown that significant health benefits can be obtained by exercising moderately. Moderately can be defined as working at perceived exertion **Levels 4 to 6** for 30 minutes in either a single session or in three separate 10-minute sessions for most, or all, days of the week.

Greater health benefits can be gained from exercising more often and with greater intensity, but you will get important gains from even this moderate program.

If your goal is fitness

Keep working until you are exerting at perceived exertion **Levels 5 to 7** for 20 to 60 minutes during each exercise session. Remember, at **Level 5** you walk as if you are **on your way to an appointment.** At **Level 7,** you walk as if you are **ten minutes late** for that appointment. Maximum is **Level 8.** Be sure to maintain speeds that keep you in your target zone. Work up gradually to five vigorous sessions per week.

If your goal is weight loss

Gradually build up to and maintain walking in your target zone for 20 miles a week. If it is difficult to stay at target for this long a time, go for distance, walking at a pace comfortable for your body. However, greater intensity is more effective for both weight reduction and maintenance of weight loss.

The math, although not much fun, is very straightforward. To burn off one pound of fat requires utilizing 3,500 Calories. To cover the distance of one mile, a 150-pound person will burn approximately 100 Calories. This certainly varies with the intensity level and even the temperature at which you are exercising! But 100 Calories serves as an approximation. So if you cover 20 miles a week, you will approximately burn:

2,000 Calories or 20 miles x 100 Calories per mile.

If you restrict your food intake another 1,400 Calories by eliminating 200 Calories per day, you'll use up nearly 3,500 Calories per week! You could lose close to a pound a week. This is a conservative and safe way to approach the "weighty" issue of weight control.

This 20-mile-per-week rule is a general guideline applicable to most people. Individuals with metabolic problems should work closely with a health care provider in a weight loss/maintenance program.

Your Shape*Walking* program will add progressive resistance training five times per week to build muscular strength.

Remember: Muscle burns more calories than fat! This is very important! On top of fitness walking and strength training, you need flexibility stretching and a sound nutritional plan.

Remember: Muscle weighs more than fat! As you build and strengthen your body's major muscle groups, you may not see a change on the scale. You may even gain weight. However, you will notice a difference in how you feel and look—strong, svelte, and energized!

Remember: For both health and fitness benefits, it is important to do some form of physical activity most days.

Making Your Fitness Walking Progression Plan

Any aerobic or heart-healthy exercise program you plan should have three elements:

Frequency—how *often* you work out

Intensity—how *hard* you exercise

Duration—how *long* your exercise session is (not including warm-up, cool-down, and stretch)

Remember to modify only one element at a time in order to progress safely and effectively. Increase your effort approximately 10 percent per week for safe progress. Start and maintain your program at a frequency of five days per week to establish the habit of frequent walking.

◆ Duration is increased first.

◆ Intensity is increased second. This allows your body to become accustomed to being exercised for longer periods of time.

Example of a Model Progression Plan

This plan is for an individual whose starting duration is 10 minutes. This can be used as a *general* guideline. But it is better to make your individual progression plan, using your own starting duration baseline.

In this model, the goal is to progress safely...

From:

  Week 1 Workout
  10 minutes per session
  5 days per week
  Intensity **Levels 5 to 6**

To:

  Week 10 Workout
  25 minutes per session
  5 days per week
  Intensity **Levels 5 to 7**

The Model Progression Chart on the next page has a start time (duration) of 10 minutes and increases duration by the 10 percent increase per week rule. That means one minute is added to the previous week's duration. If your start time is 20 minutes, then add another two minutes to raise duration by 10 percent. If your start time is 30 minutes, add three minutes, etc.

All **bold** figures in the chart indicate an increase in exercise time or intensity.

Weeks 1 to 6

Modify the length of time. Frequency of five times per week and intensity **(Levels 5 to 6)** remain the same. The duration increases approximately 10 percent per week.

Week 6

Frequency remains at five times per week. Duration remains at 18 minutes. Intensity is increased from **Levels 5 or 6 to 5 or 7.**

Weeks 7 to 10

Frequency of five times per week stays constant; intensity **(Levels 5 to 7)** stays constant. Exercise time is gradually increased at about 10 percent per week.

Model Progression Chart

Week	Exercise Time	Frequency	Intensity Level
1	10 minutes	5 X week	5–6
2	**11.5 minutes**	5 X week	5–6
3	**13 minutes**	5 X week	5–6
4	**14.5 minutes**	5 X week	5–6
5	**16 minutes**	5 X week	5–6
6	**18 minutes**	5 X week	5–6
7	18 minutes	5 X week	**5–7**
8	**20 minutes**	5 X week	5–7
9	**22.5 minutes**	5 X week	5–7
10	**25 minutes**	5 X week	5–7

All bold figures indicate an increase in exercise time or intensity.

Track your progress! Use photocopies of charts in the back of this book to help you stay on track. Charting your progress can inspire you to keep movin'!

Ready for Shaping?

The Great Shape*Walking* Benefits

Shape*Walking* is a unique and total fitness package because it adds the benefits of strength training and flexibility stretching to fitness walking. Adding resistance-strength training to your fitness walking routine will tone and shape your body. You will be shaping! In Step 1, we discussed the "overload principle." That principle reminds us that we build muscle mass and strength by challenging the muscle multiple times with progressively heavier resistance. The resistance-strength training portion of your Shape*Walking* fitness routine can further help you to:

◆ Build muscle.

◆ Increase bone strength.

◆ Fight against osteoporosis.

◆ Increase metabolic rate (muscle burns more calories than fat).

◆ Improve performance of daily living tasks.

◆ Combat frailty in the elderly.

◆ Reduce risk of injury.

◆ Improve physical appearance and posture.

◆ Provide positive mental outlook.

◆ Increase self-confidence.

Earn a Black Belt—In Shape*Walking*!

Remember Dr. Wayne L. Westcott's particularly clear definition of strength training from Step 1? "Strength training is the process of exercising with progressively heavier resistance for the purpose of strengthening the musculoskeletal system." The Shape*Walking* program exercises use differently colored, non-latex elastic bands as well as your own body weight to build strength through resistance (see pages 78-81). Your goal is to advance through the colors:

ORANGE	=	**moderate resistance**
GREEN	=	**medium resistance**
BLUE	=	**heavy resistance**
PLUM	=	**extra-heavy resistance**

When you reach the extra-heavy resistance band (plum), it's like earning your Shape*Walking* black belt.

You will perform each resistance-strength training exercise at least two, or preferably three times a week, every *other* day. It's important to have a rest day in between your strength sessions. (If it's more convenient for you to do your resistance-strength training *every* day, alternate your upper and lower body exercises. Monday—upper body exercises, Tuesday—lower body exercises, etc.)

The Mat Workout for the back and abdominal muscles is a resistance-strength/stretching routine for the trunk of your body. This workout works major muscle groups associated with the spinal column and the wall of the abdomen. It's really a continuation of the stretching and resistance-strength training components of Shape*Walking*, but it is *done on its own two days a week* with a day of rest in between.

Did you know that no bones provide support for the abdominal cavity (which houses your internal organs)? This region is supported entirely by the strength of your abdominals! So building a strong abdominal wall is key to keeping your body "together." The abdominal and back muscles work as "partners" in the proper functioning of your trunk. Strengthening these two muscle systems helps you stand straight and tall, allows you to twist or turn, and improves your posture and carriage, enabling you to walk erect. Strong abdominal muscles, in fact, directly provide support for your back and stability for your trunk. Don't forget: Strong abdominal muscles give you a flat tummy! Strong back muscles enable you to perform the lifting, carrying, pushing, and pulling tasks of your everyday life.

Getting Started with Resistance-Strength Training

Some guidelines to keep in mind before getting started on specific Shape*Walking* resistance-strength exercises:

Warm up
Always warm up for five to seven minutes before doing your Shape*Walking* band exercises. This means you must move the large muscle groups in a smooth, rhythmic pattern. Walking, biking, and slow jogging are all good warm-ups. If you have done the fitness walking portion of Shape*Walking* , it will serve as your warm-up. If not, be sure to warm up before you begin any resistance-strength training or stretching!

Do it right!
Perform each exercise slowly and smoothly. Don't jerk the Shape*Walking* band. Don't use momentum or gravity (like throwing your body weight against the band or jerking the band). Make sure your muscles are doing the work.

Check your form. Use a mirror or reflective store window. That means keeping good posture and alignment *throughout* the exercise, not just at the beginning or the end. Make sure you are balanced. Hold on to a wall to help maintain balance if necessary.

Finally, perform each resistance-strength training exercise throughout the entire range of motion that's comfortable for you. Start out counting two counts on each phase of the exercise. For example, lift for two counts, hold for two counts, and take two counts to return to starting position. As you progress, count four counts during each phase of the exercise.

Pain or fatigue

Pain is a warning that something is wrong. *Stop* immediately. Likewise, if you are exhausted or fatigued, you are overdoing it. *Stop* immediately.

You may have heard the expression, "No pain, no gain." Thankfully, those days are over in fitness circles. Anyone who thinks pain is a part of fitness training is absolutely, 100 percent, totally wrong!

Proper breathing

Breathing correctly is essential to getting results. Never, never, never hold your breath! Breathe deeply into your abdomen, filling your lungs at the beginning of each resistance exercise. Remember to exhale during the *exertion* portion of the exercise.

Keep good records

It's best to keep accurate records of your exercise time and progress. A Shape *Walking* Resistance-Strength Training Record is included at the back of the book to help you.

Cool down and stretch after your resistance-strength training session

Your muscles need to relax after being worked. Remember to cool down for five to seven minutes. Stretching after your strength session helps your muscles relax and also gives them greater flexibility.

Finding Your Starting Level and Color

Just as when you started fitness walking, you need to find your starting level for resistance-strength training. First, perform the exercise without any elastic band (no resistance) and check your form. Now try it with the orange band for 10 repetitions without a rest. The last repetition should be difficult to complete, and you should experience some muscle fatigue. If you can't do all 10 repetitions, do as many as you can. That is your starting point. If you can easily do 10 repetitions, try 12. If you can easily do 12 repetitions, try 15. If you can easily do 15 repetitions, go to the next color (green) level. Keep repeating this process until you find your starting color and starting number of repetitions. As you get stronger, progress gradually as is comfortable for your body.

For exercises that use only your body weight (no resistance band), start with 10 repetitions, or as many as you can do. Progress by moving to 12 and then 15 repetitions. To further progress, complete the advanced versions of the exercises presented in the Shape*Walking* Photo Shoot section of this book. For example, progress from wall push-ups to floor push-ups, or from the diagonal leaning lunge to the advanced backward lunge.

Every time you perform a resistance-strength exercise, it counts as a rep (short for repetition). **A rep is defined as the single and complete action of the exercise from start to finish and back to the starting position.** In order to build muscle, it's not enough to do one rep per exercise, as the muscle you are strengthening needs to be challenged repeatedly. For every exercise in this book, you should perform 10 to 15 reps, each in a row without interruption.

A set consists of a given number of complete and continuous reps of a single exercise. One set of 10 to 12 reps per exercise should be challenging enough for the mature adult. However, if you are fit, younger than 60, in good condition, or work out regularly, you might need the additional challenge of multiple sets of 10 to 15 reps per exercise.

If, after a complete workout, you find that doing one set per exercise is too easy, you can repeat the entire workout, increase the number of reps per set, or do two sets per exercise the next time. Make sure you increase the number of reps or sets gradually to prevent injury and/or exhaustion. If you haven't worked out for a long time, it's always recommended that you start off easily and slowly increase your workload.

The three tailor-made workouts—20-minute, Anti-osteoporosis, and Comprehensive—as well as the Mat Workout, begin with a "single set" of repetitions. **Remember, a set is 10, 12, or 15 repetitions of the same exercise.** If your schedule and level of vigor permit, do one to three sets of any exercise that is important to your goals as discussed above.

The Shape*Walking* Photo Shoot section in Step 6 presents explanations of each resistance-strength exercise's start and end position accompanied by photographs to help you complete each correctly.

A rep is defined as the single and complete action of the exercise from start to finish and back to the starting position.

A set consists of a given number of complete and continuous reps of a single exercise.

A set is 10, 12, or 15 repetitions of the same exercise.

Step 5

Stretching & Cool-Down

Achieving Flexibility Through Stretching

As discussed in Step 1, inactivity, injury, or certain disease states tend to decrease flexibility. Flexibility stretching:

- Increases range of motion.
- Promotes a sense of well-being.
- Relaxes mind and body.
- Reduces stiffness.
- Prevents injuries, such as muscle strains.
- Improves ability to perform daily tasks.

It is important to make flexibility stretching a part of any fitness routine. Stretching muscles helps them grow, feels good, and releases tension. Effective flexibility stretching requires warm muscles. So stretch *after* your workout. Follow this order:

1. Warm-up (five to seven minutes).
2. Walking in your target zone.
3. Cool-down (five to seven minutes)—Walk slowly to bring your heart rate down to normal.

4. Resistance-strength training.
5. Flexibility stretching.

At all times during the stretch period, *breathe* deeply and relax. Take a deep breath into your abdomen. Exhale slowly. Avoid shallow breathing.

Do not bounce. Stretch only to the point of gentle tension. Do not stretch to the point of pain.

Flexibility Stretching and Shape*Walking*

The three tailor-made workouts (explained in detail in the Shape*Walking* Photo Shoot) are:

◆ The 20-Minute Workout.

◆ The Anti-Osteoporosis Workout.

◆ The Comprehensive Workout.

Each workout includes safe stretching exercises that increase flexibility in your major muscle groups, resulting in an improved ability to perform daily tasks and also a lowered risk of injury. Each routine stretches muscle groups that you have worked during the fitness walking component of Shape*Walking* and/or "loaded" with resistance during strength training.

As discussed in Step 4, the Mat Workout consists of strengthening and stretching exercises for the back and abdominals and is an integral part of Shape*Walking*. No matter which tailor-made workout you choose, you should be doing the Mat Workout *at least two days per week.* Back problems are very common in our society and are often associated with tight back muscles. The stretching portion of the Mat Workout will stretch out your tight back muscles and give you a more supple, flexible back!

Staying on Track

Now that you are on your way, it's important to stay motivated and keep on your fitness track. Here are some tips.

Guidelines for Beginning and Experienced Shape*Walkers*

Shape*Walking* Tips

- ◆ Mix casual walking with Shape*Walking*.
- ◆ If you work very hard one day, exercise less vigorously the next.
- ◆ Vary your route and location as you become more comfortable with your exercise outings.
- ◆ Be sure you are dressed appropriately for the weather.
- ◆ Be alert to your surroundings.
- ◆ Make walking outings part of your daily routine. Find scenic and interesting paths in your area. Walk to places you normally drive to—church, the store, or a restaurant.
- ◆ Pick up a copy of *Walking* or *Prevention* magazine at your local bookstore. Read how others are staying on track.
- ◆ Consider participating in local walking events just for fun.

◆ When you feel especially energetic, add challenge and burn more calories through interval training. Interval training is increasing the level of your workout's intensity for either short periods of time or for distances. For brief intervals, say 30 seconds to two minutes, speed up and walk with more intensity or walk faster for a short distance.

◆ Another way to add challenge: Walk uphill or climb some stairs while Shape*Walking*.

Add challenge to your workout—climb stairs!

Shape*Walking at scenic Summit Ave. and Mississippi Blvd., Saint Paul, Minnesota.*

◆ Don't feel you *must* do everything by the book. Be your own coach. Use this program as a guide and feel free to mix and match other activities. For example, you may wish to substitute jogging, biking, or aerobic dance for the fitness walking component. Perhaps you want to use the weight machines at your local health club instead of the Shape*Walking* bands or to take some stretching or yoga classes.

◆ Keep track of your progress. *Use charts in the back of book!*

◆ Remember to do some form of physical activity most days of the week. But most importantly, have fun!

Johan Forsberg, on his 80th birthday.
Stavanger, Norway, 1965.
Johan Forsberg was a dentist and the grandfather of Karla Caspari, Caspari Design Group, Minneapolis, designer of this book.

Throughout most of his adult life, Mr. Forsberg closed his office for one hour each day at noon to go for a fitness walk. He worked until age 87 and died at age 96.

Resistance-strength training tips

◆ Remember to take your Shape *Walking* band along with you on your fitness walks.

◆ Also, remember to pack your Shape *Walking* gear–shoes, clothing, Shape *Walking* book and band–when you travel.

◆ Do your resistance-strength training program three times a week, separated by rest days.

◆ Remember to breathe deeply into your abdomen, filling your lungs at the beginning of each resistance exercise. Remember to exhale during the *exertion* portion of the exercise.

◆ Work toward your Shape*Walking* black belt (highest resistance), progressing gradually and safely through orange, green, blue, and plum. (Ordering information for Shape*Walking* bands is on the last page.)

◆ The three tailor-made workouts, 20-minute, Anti-osteoporosis, and Comprehensive, begin with a single set of repetitions. *A set is 10, 12, or 15 repetitions of the same exercise.* If your schedule permits, do one to three sets of any exercise that is important to your goals.

Flexibility stretching tips:

◆ Remember to stretch out at the end of your Shape*Walking* program.

◆ Do not bounce! Do not stretch to the point of pain!

◆ If you are doing only fitness walking at this time, stretch out at the end of your walk.

◆ If you have added strength training, stretch out after your complete workout.

Flexibility stretching should always be done after your muscles are warm—after fitness walking or resistance-strength training. For variety change the order of your program:

◆ **Full Program:** warm-up, fitness walking, cool-down, resistance-strength training, flexibility stretching.

◆ **Resistance-Strength Training:** warm-up, resistance-strength training, cool-down, flexibility stretching.

◆ **Interval Training:** warm-up, fitness walking, portion of resistance-strength training, fitness walking, portion of resistance-strength training, cool-down, flexibility stretching.

Hydration is very important

◆ Drink adequate liquids to ensure that you do not become dehydrated as a protection for your health.

◆ Drink two to three 8-ounce glasses of fluid up to two hours prior to your exercise outing.

◆ Ten minutes before your outing, drink one to two 8-ounce glasses of water.

◆ Coffee, tea, pop containing caffeine, beer, and alcohol dehydrate the body. *Do not* count them as part of your daily fluid intake.

◆ During your exercise session, drink as much as you can, ideally, 8-10 ounces every 20 minutes.

◆ Drink even more than this to replace fluids lost during vigorous exercise.

◆ Drink at least six to eight 8-ounce glasses of fluid, water, sports drinks, and diluted juices per day for overall health.

◆ Drink *before* you get thirsty! Your brain signals thirst *after* significant dehydration.

◆ After exercise, drink to satisfy your thirst—and then some!

◆ Juices, especially orange or orange/banana blend, replace carbohydrates and potassium lost during exercise.

Excerpted from: "Fluids, Dehydration and Thirst Quenchers," Nancy Clark, M.S., R.D., *Sports Medicine Brookline*, Brookline, MA 02167.

Recent medical studies have shown that fitness walking is safe, highly effective, and prolongs life. However, from time to time, replace fitness walking with another aerobic exercise, such as step aerobics, biking, etc., for variety.

Most Importantly…Have Fun!

Shape*Walking* Photo Shoot

Introduction

You have now been introduced to the highly versatile Shape*Walking* program. As previously discussed, any effective fitness program must contain three specific components:

◆ Aerobic/heart-healthy exercise

◆ Resistance-strength training

◆ Flexibility stretching

To meet this requirement, Shape*Walking*'s three major components are:

◆ Fitness walking.

◆ Resistance-strength training, with your own body weight and/or a resistance band.

◆ Safe flexibility stretching.

Remember: You may mix and match the three components of Shape*Walking* with other fitness options. For example, you may want to replace fitness walking with step aerobics or yoga for the stretching component as fits your schedule and your fancy!

This section presents a Photo Shoot—a combination of photos and instructions—of your Shape*Walking* program. You will choose one tailor-made workout depending on your schedule and your goals. You may choose one of the following:

◆ The 20-minute Workout

◆ The Anti-osteoporosis Workout

◆ The Comprehensive Workout

The Photo Shoot presents photographs of all the exercises in each workout to guide you in using proper form. There is one photograph of each stretch exercise. Resistance-strength training exercises are shown in both starting and ending positions.

Since fitness walking and the Mat Workout are integral to all three workouts, photographs of these components are presented first. Next, for easy reference, all resistance-strength exercises and stretches that belong to each workout are presented together as one section. The Photo Shoot sections are organized for easy reference:

◆ Fitness Walking

◆ The Mat Workout

◆ The 20-minute Workout

◆ The Anti-osteoporosis Workout

◆ The Comprehensive Workout

Since stretching is performed on warm muscles, the resistance-strength training photographs are presented first; the photographs of the stretches are presented second.

Guidelines

For all programs, fitness walking is the heart-healthy component of your exercise program. Walk vigorously (mostly at target zone) five days per week. Further, it is best to add the Mat Workout for abdominals and back, at least two days per week, to all workouts.

Shape*Walking* consists of three complete workouts. You will choose the one that is right for you. Each workout consists of a resistance-strength training component and a matching stretching component that is done three times per week spaced by a rest day or by the Mat Workout. The Mat Workout also consists of resistance-strength training and stretching and is done two days a week minimum. Don't skip the Mat Workout! It is an extremely important component needed to complete your fitness program.

Reminder: You should always do some form of exercise most days of the week.

As an example, if you feel the Anti-osteoporosis Workout is best for you, try the following model schedule:

Monday	Anti-osteoporosis Workout
Tuesday	Mat Workout
Wednesday	Anti-osteoporosis Workout
Thursday	Mat Workout
Friday	Anti-osteoporosis Workout
Saturday	Some form of moderate exercise
Sunday	Some form of moderate exercise

Fitness walking at your target zone—five days each week!

Two charts are included to help you keep track of and record your progress:

◆ Fitness Walking Record
◆ Shape*Walking* Resistance-Strength Training Chart

Photo Shoot: Fitness Walking Workout

Proper Fitness Walking Technique

Stretches

To be performed on days when you do not include strength training in your program.

- Lateral Neck Stretch
- Lateral Shoulder Stretch
- Pectoral Stretch
- Hip Flexor Stretch
- Inner Thigh Stretch
- Hamstring Stretch
    - Low
    - Elevated
- Quadriceps Stretch
- Calf Stretch

Proper Fitness Walking Technique

For proper posture:

◆ Stand tall with head held high.

◆ Hold body erect, head up. Keep eyes looking ahead. Keep chin straight, parallel to the ground, and not jutting forward.

◆ Draw an imaginary straight line connecting ear, shoulder, hip, knee, and ankle down each side of the body.

◆ Do not bend at the waist or slouch at the shoulder. Check your posture in a mirror or the reflective glass in a store window as you walk past.

Arm movement and position are important

Casey Meyers describes well the proper arm movement in his book, *Walking:*

◆ Hold your hands in loose, closed fists with your thumbs resting on top of your fingers.

◆ Bend your arms 90 degrees at the elbow.

◆ Pump your bent arms vigorously back and forth, but naturally—do not cross the front midline of your body.

◆ Swing your arms forward, no higher than your breast while holding your arms close to the body.

◆ Swing your arms back so that your closed fists meet the side seam of your pants.

◆ Keep your shoulders relaxed and square. Leg movement and position propel you.

◆ Your legs should swing forward naturally with your leg almost fully extended.

Foot placement is very important

◆ Land with a heel strike with the foot of your leading leg.

◆ Strike with the heel; allow the foot to roll from heel to toe.

◆ Push off from the ball of your trailing foot *(toe-off)*. The foot placement path should form two straight, narrow parallel lines.

Hip motion is a natural movement

◆ Allow your pelvis to have a natural forward and backward motion.

◆ Do not swing hips from side to side.

◆ Keep your hips relaxed.

Breathing correctly helps endurance

◆ Breathe deeply down into your abdomen.

◆ Allow the air to completely fill your lungs.

◆ Avoid shallow breathing or panting.

◆ Exhale, flattening your tummy.

Technique for increased speed

◆ Pump your bent arms vigorously.

◆ Shorten stride length–take short, quick steps.

Walk Tall

1. Head erect, eyes forward, chin parallel to ground.
2. Shoulder square.
3. Elbow back, bent 90 degrees.
4. Toe push.
5. Heel strike.
6. Hand in loose fist.

Fitness walking at historic Summit Ave. and Mississippi Blvd., Saint Paul, Minnesota.

Remember to stretch after you've completed your fitness walking.

The following pages provide suggested stretches to use on the days when you are fitness walking without your chosen strength and stretching workout.

Photo Shoot: Fitness Walking Workout

Stretches

To be performed on days when you do not include a strength and stretching workout.

Lateral Neck Stretch
Lateral Shoulder Stretch
Pectoral Stretch
Hip Flexor Stretch
Inner Thigh Stretch
Hamstring Stretch
    Low
    Elevated
Quadriceps Stretch
Calf Stretch

Starting position for standing stretches:
Start all standing stretches using proper posture: ears, shoulders, hips, knees aligned; chin parallel to the ground; abdominals in, knees soft, shoulders relaxed.

Lateral Neck Stretch
While maintaining good posture (ear aligned with shoulder), bend your head sideways (ear toward shoulder). Initially, hold for 10 seconds; release and stretch more deeply for 30 seconds. Total stretch time: 40 seconds. *This stretch should be felt along the side of the neck.*
Repeat on opposite side.

Lateral Shoulder Stretch

Gently pull elbow down and toward midline of back. Initially, hold for 10 seconds; release and stretch more deeply for 30 seconds. Total stretch time: 40 seconds. *This stretch should be felt along the outside shoulder area.*

Repeat on other side.

Pectoral Stretch

Place hands palms up on your shoulders. Pull shoulder blades down and together in one motion while bringing elbows back with arms bent at elbows. *Feel a gentle stretch along the front of the shoulders.* Initially, hold for 10 seconds; release and stretch more deeply for 30 seconds.

Total stretch time: 40 seconds.

Hip Flexor Stretch

Place one leg in front of the other, with the knee of the forward leg slightly bent. Keep your lower back straight. Tighten buttocks and abdominal muscles. Press hips forward to *feel stretch along the front of the hip*. Initially, hold for 10 seconds; release and stretch more deeply for 30 seconds. Total stretch time: 40 seconds.

Repeat on other side.

Inner Thigh Stretch

Keep your back upright. Bring feet into a wide stance (slightly wider than shoulder width). Move left leg (knee bent) to the left to stretch right inner thigh. Press right leg toward ground to *feel stretch along inside of right leg*. Repeat on the right side to stretch left inner thigh. Initially, hold for 10 seconds; release and stretch more deeply for 30 seconds. Total stretch time: 40 seconds.

Repeat on other side.

Hamstring Stretch
Low

With your back straight, bend forward at the hips and place weight on back leg, move one leg forward, heel on the ground. Press forward leg gently toward ground. Flex foot of the forward leg up to exaggerate the stretch. Initially, hold for 10 seconds; release and stretch more deeply for 30 seconds. Total stretch time: 40 seconds. *This stretch should be felt along the back of the thigh.*

Repeat with opposite leg.

or

Elevated

Stand with your lower back straight and one foot on a stool. Then lean forward at the hip. Do not round your back. Initially, hold for 10 seconds; release and stretch more deeply for 30 seconds. Total stretch time: 40 seconds. *This stretch should be felt along the back of the thigh.*

Repeat on opposite side.

Quadriceps Stretch

Standing upright, bring your heel to your buttocks by grasping the foot with whichever hand is comfortable for your body. Do not lean forward at waist. Initially, hold for 10 seconds; release and stretch more deeply for 30 seconds. Total stretch time: 40 seconds. *This stretch should be felt along the front of the thigh.*

Repeat on opposite side.

Calf Stretch

With your toes pointing forward, lean forward. Keep your body straight with your heels on the floor. Maintain arch in foot. Perform with knee of back leg straight to *feel a gentle stretch in the calf.* Initially, hold for 10 seconds; release and stretch more deeply for 30 seconds. Total stretch time: 40 seconds.

Repeat on opposite side.

Photo Shoot: Mat Workout

Strength Training

Forward Curl for Abdominals
Reverse Curl for Abdominals
Diagonal Curl
Back Extension
Upper Back Arm Extension
Lower Back Leg Extension

Stretches

Diagonal Hip Stretch
Single Knee to Chest Stretch
Double Knee to Chest Stretch
Trunk Extension
Trunk Rotation

Mat Workout

The Mat Workout should be performed a minimum of two days per week, separated by a rest day.

Mat Workout:

- Strengthens and stretches your back and abdominal muscle groups.
- Counteracts back pain.
- Lowers your risk of back injuries.
- Stabilizes and improves the flexibility of your trunk.
- Improves your ability to perform daily tasks of life such as lifting, pushing, and pulling.
- Improves your appearance, your posture, and your self-confidence.
- Combats osteoporosis in the spine.
- Builds muscle.
- Increases bone strength.
- Increases metabolic rate (muscle burns more calories than fat).
- Combats frailty in the elderly.
- Provides positive mental outlook.

Photo Shoot: Mat Workout

Strength Training

Forward Curl for Abdominals
Reverse Curl for Abdominals
Diagonal Curl
Back Extension
Upper Back Arm Extension
Lower Back Leg Extension

Forward Curl for Abdominals

Lie on your back with fingers interlaced behind your head. Tighten abdominal muscles, then lift head and shoulders off the ground. Be careful not to pull on your neck with your hands.

REMEMBER: Lifting = 2 beats; holding = 2 beats; returning = 2 beats. In time, progress to 4 beats each.

Reverse Curl for Abdominals

Lie on your back with knees bent up. Tighten abdominal muscles and use them to pull or rock the pelvis, resulting in the knees moving toward the chest.

REMEMBER: Lifting = 2 beats; holding = 2 beats; returning = 2 beats. In time, progress to 4 beats each.

Diagonal Curl for Abdominals

Lie on your back with fingers interlaced behind your head. Tighten abdominal muscles and bring one shoulder up toward the opposite knee so that the shoulder blade comes off the floor. Opposite shoulder remains down. Repeat with the other shoulder. Be careful not to pull on the neck with your hands.

REMEMBER: Lifting = 2 beats; holding = 2 beats; returning = 2 beats. In time, progress to 4 beats each.

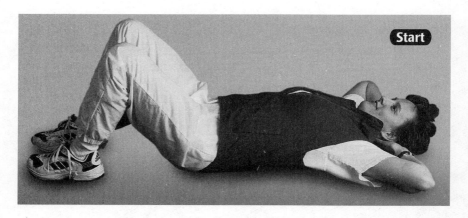

Back Extension

While lying on your stomach with your arms at your sides, arch your back, lifting your chest off the floor.

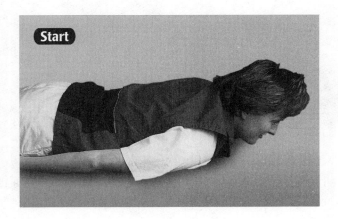

REMEMBER: **Lifting = 2 beats; holding = 2 beats; returning = 2 beats. In time, progress to 4 beats each.**

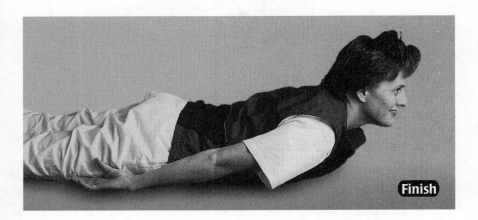

Upper Back Arm Extension

On all fours, tuck your tummy in so your back is flat like a table top. Lift one arm in the air in front of you. *Do not allow back to arch.* Repeat on the other side.

REMEMBER: Lifting = 2 beats; holding = 2 beats; returning = 2 beats. In time, progress to 4 beats each.

Lower Back Leg Extension

On all fours, tuck your tummy in so your back is flat like a table top. Extend one leg behind you, parallel to the floor. Now use your back and buttocks to lift the leg up from its starting position. *Do not allow back to arch.* Repeat with the other leg.

REMEMBER: Lifting = 2 beats; holding = 2 beats; returning = 2 beats. In time, progress to 4 beats each.

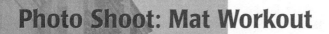

Photo Shoot: Mat Workout

Stretches

Diagonal Hip Stretch
Single Knee to Chest Stretch
Double Knee to Chest Stretch
Trunk Extension
Trunk Rotation

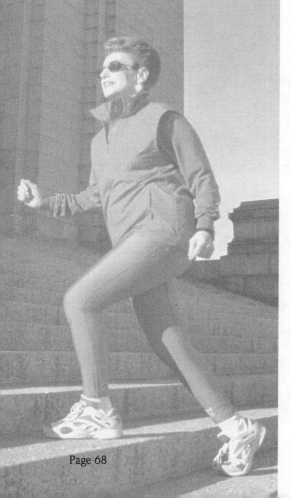

Diagonal Hip Stretch

Lying on your back, grasp your right knee with your left hand and gently bring it toward the left shoulder. *Feel a gentle stretch along the outside of the right hip.* Initially, hold for 10 seconds; release and stretch more deeply for 30 seconds. Total stretch time: 40 seconds.

Repeat on other side.

Single Knee to Chest Stretch

Lying on your back, bring one knee up and gently hug it to your chest. *Feel a gentle stretch along the back of the raised thigh and in the lower back.* Opposite knee should be slightly bent. Initially, hold for 10 seconds; release and stretch more deeply for 30 seconds. Total stretch time: 40 seconds.

Repeat on other side.

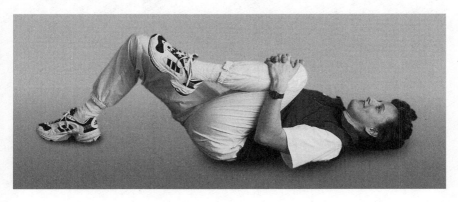

Double Knee to Chest Stretch

Lying on back, bring both knees up and gently hug them to your chest. *Feel a gentle stretch along the back of both thighs and in the lower back.* Initially, hold for 10 seconds; release and stretch

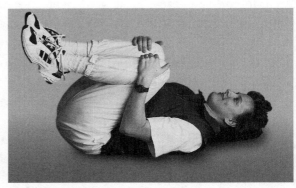

more deeply for 30 seconds. Total stretch time: 40 seconds.

Trunk Extension

While lying on your stomach, place your hands next to your shoulders. Extend your arms by straightening the elbows. (Some ShapeWalkers will be unable to straighten the elbows all the way. That's OK. Only go as far as you can to feel a good stretch.) *Feel a gentle stretch in your lower back.* Initially, hold for 10 seconds; release and stretch more deeply for 30 seconds. Total stretch time: 40 seconds.

Trunk Rotation

Lie on your back with knees bent. Allow the knees to fall gently to one side while keeping your knees together. *Feel a gentle stretch in the middle part of the back.* Initially, hold for 10 seconds; release and stretch more deeply for 30 seconds. Total stretch time: 40 seconds.

Repeat on other side.

Designed with You in Mind...

Three Tailor-Made Workouts

Here now are the workout choices previously introduced to you. As discussed, you will choose the one best suited to your goals and time schedule. Each was designed with you in mind...

20-minute Workout: This resistance-strength and flexibility stretching workout emphasizes major muscles of the upper and lower body. It is designed to give a well-rounded strength building and stretching workout in only 20 minutes. This program should be performed three times per week spaced by the Mat Workout or one rest day.

Anti-osteoporosis Workout: This resistance-strength and flexibility stretching workout is designed to strengthen the major muscles of the upper and lower body *plus* strengthen the specific bones most affected by osteoporosis. Bone is a dynamic structure. This means it responds to *loading* or stress by becoming stronger. Since muscles are attached to bones, using external resistance plus body weight to strengthen the muscles is a great way to load the bone to make it stronger. This program should be performed three times per week spaced by the Mat Workout or one rest day. This workout is designed as a preventive workout for osteoporosis.

Comprehensive Workout: The Comprehensive Workout contains all the components of the 20-minute and the Anti-osteoporosis Workouts plus supplementary stretching and strengthening exercises. You can either choose to perform this workout on those days when you have more time or choose specific exercises from this program to meet your unique fitness needs. However you use it, this program should be performed three times per week spaced by the Mat Workout or one rest day.

Photo Shoot: 20-Minute Workout

Strength Training

Heel Raise
Diagonal Leaning Lunge
Mini-squat with Band
Biceps with Band
Triceps with Band
Upper Back Builder
Wall Push-up
    Hands Wide
    Hands Narrow
Hip Series with Band
    Outer Thigh
    Quadriceps
    Inner Thigh
    Diagonal Buttocks
    Buttocks Extension

Stretches

Lateral Neck Stretch
Lateral Shoulder Stretch
Pectoral Stretch
Hip Flexor Stretch
Inner Thigh Stretch
Hamstring Stretch
    Low
    Elevated
Quadriceps Stretch
Calf Stretch

20-Minute Workout

This resistance-strength and flexibility stretching program emphasizes major muscles of the upper and lower body. It is designed to give a well-rounded strength building and stretching workout in only 20 minutes. This program should be performed three times per week spaced by the Mat Workout or one rest day.

Photo Shoot: 20-Minute Workout

Strength Training

Heel Raise
Diagonal Leaning Lunge
Mini-squat with Band
Biceps with Band
Triceps with Band
Upper Back Builder
Wall Push-up
    Hands Wide
    Hands Narrow
Hip Series with Band
    Outer Thigh
    Quadriceps
    Inner Thigh
    Diagonal Buttocks
    Buttocks Extension

Heel Raise

Raise both heels off the floor, then slowly lower heels to the floor. Progress to one foot, placing the opposite foot behind ankle of foot to be raised. Repeat with opposite foot.

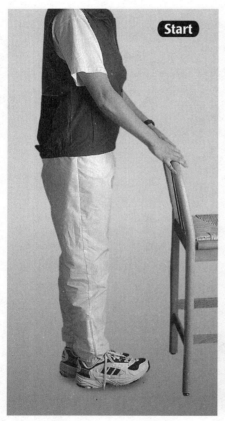
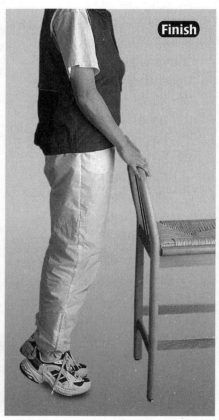

REMEMBER: Lifting = 2 beats; holding = 2 beats; returning = 2 beats. In time, progress to 4 beats each.

Diagonal Leaning Lunge

Bring one leg forward with that foot turned out diagonally 45 degrees. While maintaining an erect torso, bend the knee of the forward leg until the knee is over the foot. Hold 2 beats and return to starting position. Repeat with opposite leg. Progress to the advanced backward lunge. (See comprehensive program.)

REMEMBER: Forward motion = 2 beats; returning = 2 beats; holding = 2 beats. In time, progress to 4 beats each.

Mini-squat with Band

Stand on band and bend knees. Grasping the band in each hand, straighten slowly against resistance of band. Maintain upright posture throughout exercise. Progress to one-leg squats with band. (See Comprehensive Program.)

REMEMBER: Upward motion = 2 beats; holding = 2 beats; returning = 2 beats. In time, progress to 4 beats each.

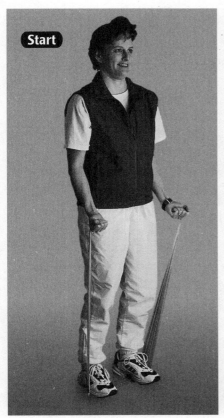

Biceps with Band

Stand on band and grasp ends of band with palms facing forward. Keep elbows stationary and next to your sides. Bring hands toward shoulders, bending elbows.

REMEMBER: Lifting = 2 beats; holding = 2 beats; returning = 2 beats. In time, progress to 4 beats each.

Triceps with Band

Grasp band as for biceps exercise, but with palms facing body. Bring elbows slightly behind the body and hold them stationary. Extend the forearms back, bringing hands in line with elbows.

REMEMBER: Extending motion = 2 beats; holding = 2 beats; returning = 2 beats. In time, progress to 4 beats each.

Upper Back Builder

Stand on band and grasp ends in each hand. Point thumbs up. Raise arms to form a 45-degree angle. Stay below shoulder level.

REMEMBER: Lifting = 2 beats; holding = 2 beats; returning = 2 beats. In time, progress to 4 beats each.

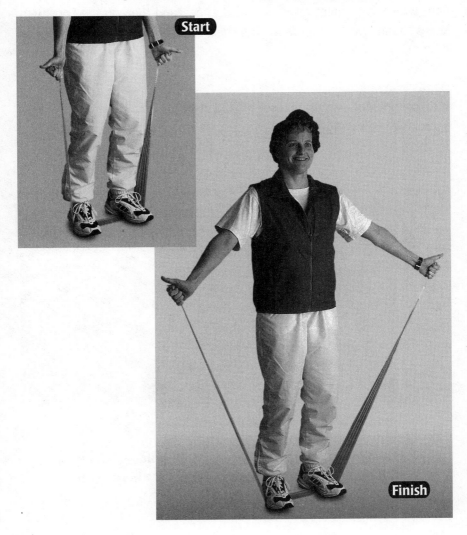

Wall Push-up

With body aligned (ears, shoulders, hips, and knees in line), perform standing push-ups against the wall. Be certain that back is not allowed to sag and head is not allowed to drop forward in front of the shoulders. Start at arms-length from the wall. Move forward smoothly toward the wall, bending elbows outward. Progress to hands on a counter top, then on the floor with body weight resting on bent knees, and then on the floor with knees straight pushing off from your toes. Hand placement will determine the muscles used.

Hands Wide

Works shoulders, chest muscles, and triceps. Place hands on wall approximately shoulder-width apart. Hands are tilted toward one another.

 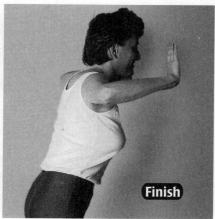

REMEMBER: Forward motion = 2 beats; holding = 2 beats; returning = 2 beats. In time, progress to 4 beats each.

Hands Narrow

Emphasizes triceps strengthening. Place hands on wall with hands in front of your face. Place your left and right hands next to one another forming a triangle with your index fingers and thumbs.

REMEMBER: **Forward motion = 2 beats; holding = 2 beats; returning = 2 beats. In time, progress to 4 beats each.**

Hip Series with Band

For best results, complete this full series of five exercises one foot at a time.

Outer Thigh

Tie band into a six- to eight-inch loop and place it around your ankles. Your feet should be shoulder-width apart. Keep one foot stationary and bring opposite foot to the side. Touch foot to ground and return to starting position. Repeat with opposite foot.

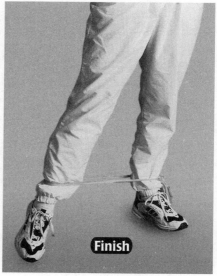

REMEMBER: Side motion = 2 beats; holding = 2 beats; returning = 2 beats. In time, progress to 4 beats each.

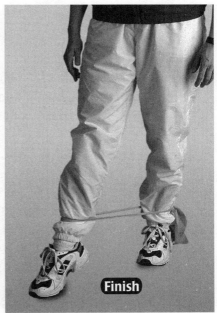

Quadriceps

Spread feet apart until the band is taut (about shoulder width). Keep one foot stationary; bring the opposite leg forward by placing the foot directly in front of its original position. Touch the forward foot down and return to resting position. Repeat with opposite foot.

REMEMBER: Forward motion = 2 beats; holding = 2 beats; returning = 2 beats. In time, progress to 4 beats each.

Inner Thigh

Place normally spaced feet in loop of band. Keep one foot stationary; turn opposite foot out diagonally 45 degrees. Bring that foot forward diagonally so it crosses in front of stationary foot. Repeat with opposite foot.

REMEMBER: Diagonal motion = 2 beats; holding = 2 beats; returning = 2 beats. In time, progress to 4 beats each.

Diagonal Buttocks

Place normally spaced feet in loop of band. Bring one foot out diagonally to the side and back. Keep abdominals tight throughout. Repeat with opposite foot.

REMEMBER: Diagonal motion = 2 beats; holding = 2 beats; returning = 2 beats. In time, progress to 4 beats each.

Buttocks Extension

In the last exercise of the hip band series, bring one foot straight behind its original position. Keep abdominals tight throughout. Repeat with opposite foot.

REMEMBER: Backward motion = 2 beats; holding = 2 beats; returning = 2 beats. In time, progress to 4 beats each.

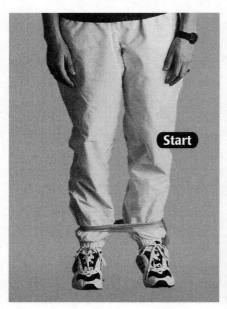

Photo Shoot: 20-Minute Workout

Stretches

Lateral Neck Stretch
Lateral Shoulder Stretch
Pectoral Stretch
Hip Flexor Stretch
Inner Thigh Stretch
Hamstring Stretch
    Low
    Elevated
Quadriceps Stretch
Calf Stretch

Starting position for standing stretches

Start all standing stretches using proper posture: ears, shoulders, hips, knees aligned; chin parallel to the ground; abdominals in; knees soft; shoulders relaxed.

Lateral Neck Stretch

While maintaining good posture (ear aligned with shoulder), bend your head sideways (ear toward shoulder). Initially, hold for 10 seconds; release and stretch more deeply for 30 seconds. Total stretch time: 40 seconds. *This stretch should be felt along the side of the neck.*

Repeat on opposite side.

Lateral Shoulder Stretch

Gently pull elbow down and toward midline of back. Initially, hold for 10 seconds; release and stretch more deeply for 30 seconds. Total stretch time: 40 seconds. *This stretch should be felt along the outside shoulder.* Repeat on other side.

Pectoral Stretch

Place hands palms up on your shoulders. Pull shoulder blades down and together in one motion while bringing elbows back with arms bent at elbows. *Feel a gentle stretch along the front of the shoulders.* Initially, hold for 10 seconds; release and stretch more deeply for 30 seconds. Total stretch time: 40 seconds.

Hip Flexor Stretch

Place one leg in front of the other, with the knee of the forward leg slightly bent. Keep your lower back straight. Tighten buttocks. Press hips forward. *Feel stretch along the front of the hip.* Initially, hold for 10 seconds; release and stretch more deeply for 30 seconds. Total stretch time: 40 seconds.

Repeat on other side.

Inner Thigh Stretch

Keep your back upright. Move left leg (knee bent) to the left to stretch right inner thigh. Press right leg toward ground. *Feel a stretch along inside of right leg.* Repeat on the right side to stretch left inner thigh. Initially, hold for 10 seconds; release and stretch more deeply for 30 seconds. Total stretch time: 40 seconds.

Repeat on other side.

Hamstring Stretch
Low

With your back straight and weight on back leg, move one leg forward, heel on ground. Press forward leg gently toward ground. Flex foot of the forward leg up to exaggerate the stretch. Initially, hold for 10 seconds; release and stretch more deeply for 30 seconds. Total stretch time: 40 seconds. *This stretch should be felt along the back of the thigh.*

Repeat with opposite leg.

or

Elevated

Stand with your lower back straight and one foot on a stool. Then lean forward at the hip. Do not round your back. Initially, hold for 10 seconds; release and stretch more deeply for 30 seconds. Total stretch time: 40 seconds. *This stretch should be felt along the back of the thigh.*

Repeat on opposite side.

Quadriceps Stretch

Standing upright, bring your heel to your buttocks by grasping the foot Whichever hand as is comfortable for your body. Do not lean forward at waist. Initially, hold for 10 seconds; release and stretch more deeply for 30 seconds. Total stretch time: 40 seconds. *This stretch should be felt along the front of the thigh.*

Repeat on opposite side.

Calf Stretch

With your toes pointing forward, lean forward. Keep your body straight with your heels on the floor. Maintain arch in foot. Perform with knee of back leg straight. *Feel a gentle stretch in the calf.* Initially, hold for 10 seconds; release and stretch more deeply for 30 seconds. Total stretch time: 40 seconds.

Repeat on opposite side.

Photo Shoot: Anti-Osteoporosis Workout

Strength Training

Heel Raise
Diagonal Leaning Lunge
Mini-squat with Band
Trunk Side Bend
Biceps with Band
Triceps with Band
Upper Back Builder
Wall Push-up
    Hands Wide
    Hands Narrow
Wrist Flexion
Wrist Extension
Hip Series with Band
    Outer Thigh
    Quadriceps
    Inner Thigh
    Diagonal Buttocks
    Buttocks Extension

Inner Thigh Stretch
Hamstring Stretch
    Low
    Elevated
Quadriceps Stretch
Calf Stretch
Wrist Flexor Stretch
Wrist Extensor Stretch

Stretches

Lateral Neck Stretch
Lateral Shoulder Stretch
Pectoral Stretch
Hip Flexor Stretch
Trunk Side Bend
Standing Trunk Rotation

Anti-Osteoporosis Workout

This resistance-strength and flexibility stretching workout is designed to strengthen the major muscles of the upper and lower body *plus* strengthen the specific bones most affected by osteoporosis. Bone is a dynamic structure. This means it responds to *loading* or stress by becoming stronger. Since muscles are attached to bones, using external resistance plus body weight to strengthen the muscles is a great way to load the bone to make it stronger. This program should be performed three times per week, spaced by the Mat Workout or one rest day.

This program is designed as a preventive program for osteoporosis. If you have been diagnosed with osteoporosis, consult with your physician before starting this or any other exercise program.

Shape *Walking* offers some particularly helpful exercises for participants diagnosed with osteoporosis:

- ◆ Fitness walking emphasizes good walking posture. By standing tall and erect, you actually extend your spine.

- ◆ Wall push-ups strengthen shoulders, chest muscles, and triceps.

- ◆ The back extension strength training and stretching exercises in the Mat Workout extend your trunk and build your back muscles.

- ◆ The wrist flexion and extension strength and stretch exercises in the Anti-osteoporosis Workout strengthen and stretch your wrists.

If you have been diagnosed with osteoporosis, modify your Anti-osteoporosis Workout as follows.

Do not perform the following:
Strength Training
- Trunk Side Bend
- Hip Series—Inner Thigh, Outer Thigh

Stretches
- Trunk Side Bend
- Standing Trunk Rotation

If you have been diagnosed with osteoporosis, modify your Mat Workout as follows.

Eliminate:
Strength Training
- Forward Curl
- Diagonal Curl
- Reverse Curl

Stretches
- Single Knee to Chest
- Double Knee to Chest
- Trunk Rotation

Emphasize:
Increased repetitions of
- Back Extension
- Upper Back Arm Extension
- Lower Back Leg Extension

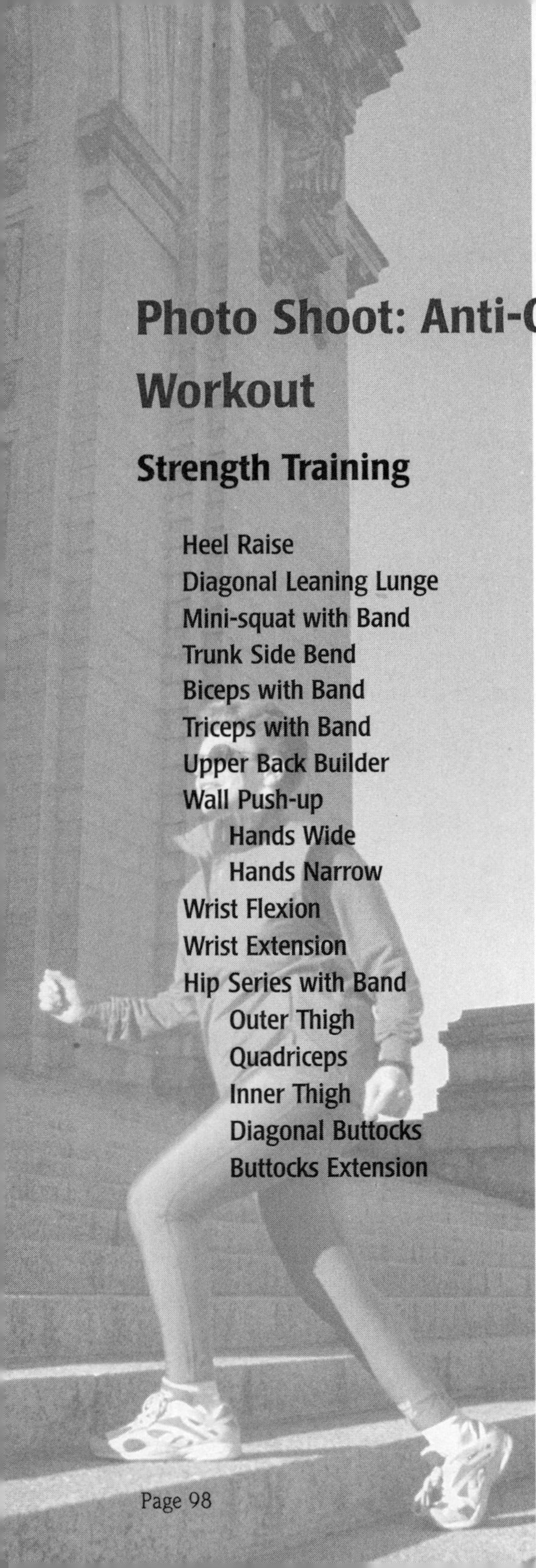

Photo Shoot: Anti-Osteoporosis Workout

Strength Training

Heel Raise
Diagonal Leaning Lunge
Mini-squat with Band
Trunk Side Bend
Biceps with Band
Triceps with Band
Upper Back Builder
Wall Push-up
    Hands Wide
    Hands Narrow
Wrist Flexion
Wrist Extension
Hip Series with Band
    Outer Thigh
    Quadriceps
    Inner Thigh
    Diagonal Buttocks
    Buttocks Extension

Heel Raise

Raise both heels off the floor, then slowly lower heels to the floor. Progress to one foot, placing the opposite foot behind ankle of foot to be raised. Repeat with opposite foot.

REMEMBER: Lifting = 2 beats; holding = 2 beats; returning = 2 beats. In time, progress to 4 beats each.

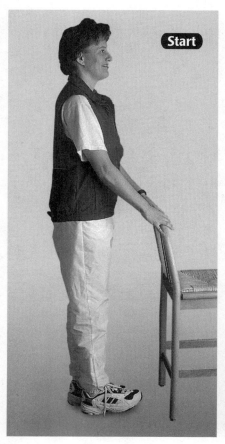
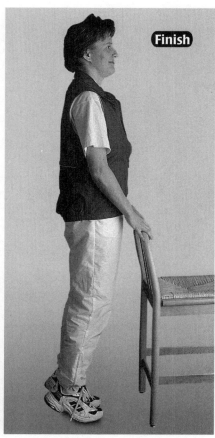

Diagonal Leaning Lunge

Bring one leg forward with that foot turned out diagonally 45 degrees. While maintaining an erect torso, bend the knee of the forward leg until the knee is over the foot. Hold 2 beats and return to starting position. Repeat with opposite leg. Progress to advanced backward lunge. (See cCmprehensive Program.)

REMEMBER: Forward motion = 2 beats; holding = 2 beats; returning = 2 beats. In time, progress to 4 beats each.

Mini-squat with Band

Stand on band and bend knees. Grasping the band in each hand, straighten slowly against resistance of band. Maintain upright posture throughout exercise. Progress to performing one-leg squats. (See Comprehensive Program.)

REMEMBER: Upward motion = 2 beats; holding = 2 beats; returning = 2 beats. In time, progress to 4 beats each.

Trunk Side Bend

Stand on band with one foot. Grasp band in hand. Bend in opposite direction against resistance of band. Keep back in line with hips. Repeat on opposite side.

REMEMBER: Leaning motion = 2 beats; holding = 2 beats; returning = 2 beats. In time, progress to 4 beats each.

Biceps with Band

Stand on band and grasp ends of band, palms facing forward. Keep elbows stationary and next to your sides. Bring hands toward shoulders, bending elbows.

REMEMBER: Lifting = 2 beats; holding = 2 beats; returning = 2 beats. In time, progress to 4 beats each.

Triceps with Band

Grasp band as for biceps exercise, but with palms facing body. Bring elbows slightly behind the body and hold them stationary. Extend the forearms back, bringing hands in line with elbows.

REMEMBER: Extending motion = 2 beats; holding = 2 beats; returning = 2 beats. In time, progress to 4 beats each.

Upper Back Builder

Stand on band, and grasp ends in each hand. Point thumbs up. Raise arms to form a 45 degree angle. Stay below shoulder level.

REMEMBER: Lifting = 2 beats; holding = 2 beats; returning = 2 beats. In time, progress to 4 beats each.

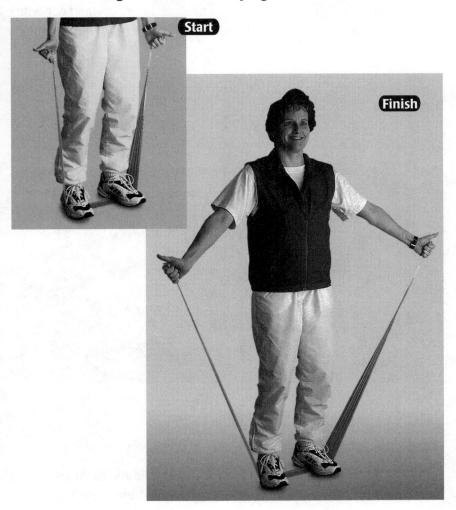

Wall Push-up

With body aligned (ears, shoulders, hips, and knees in line), perform standing push-ups against the wall. Be certain that back is not allowed to sag and head is not allowed to drop forward in front of the shoulders. Start at arms-length from the wall. Move forward smoothly toward the wall, bending elbows outward. Progress to hands on a counter top, then on the floor with body weight resting on bent knees, and then on the floor with knees straight pushing off from your toes. Hand placement will determine the muscles used.

Hands Wide

Works shoulders, chest muscles, and triceps. Place hands on wall approximately shoulder-width apart. Hands are tilted toward one another.

REMEMBER: Forward motion = 2 beats; holding = 2 beats; returning = 2 beats. In time, progress to 4 beats each.

Hands Narrow

Emphasizes triceps strengthening. Place hands on wall with hands in front of your face. Place your left and right hands next to one another forming a triangle with your index fingers and thumbs.

REMEMBER: Forward motion = 2 beats; holding = 2 beats; returning = 2 beats. In time, progress to 4 beats each.

Wrist Flexion

Hold band in one hand with palm up and hand and wrist bent down. Stand on the other end of band. Curl wrist up to *neutral* (hand and wrist aligned with forearm). Repeat with opposite hand.

REMEMBER: Lifting = 2 beats; holding = 2 beats; returning = 2 beats. In time, progress to 4 beats each.

 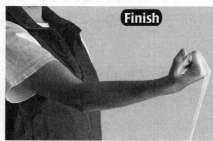

Wrist Extension

Hold band in one hand with palm down and hand and wrist aligned with forearm. Stand on the other end of the band. Bring wrist up. Repeat with opposite hand.

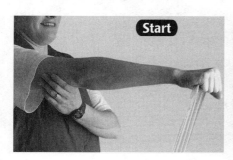 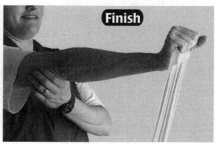

REMEMBER: Lifting = 2 beats; holding = 2 beats; returning = 2 beats. In time, progress to 4 beats each.

Hip Series with Band

For best results, complete this full series of five exercises one foot at a time.

Outer Thigh

Tie band into a six- to eight-inch loop and place it around your ankles. Your feet should be shoulder-width apart. Keep one foot stationary and bring opposite foot to the side. Touch foot to ground and return to starting position. Repeat with opposite foot

REMEMBER: Side motion = 2 beats; holding = 2 beats; returning = 2 beats. In time, progress to 4 beats each.

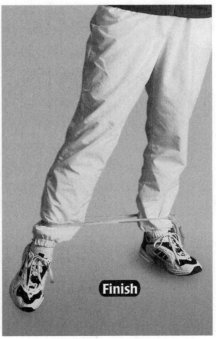

Quadriceps

Spread feet apart until the band is taut (about shoulder width). Keep one foot stationary; bring the opposite leg forward by placing the foot directly in front of its original position. Touch the forward foot down and return to resting position. Repeat with opposite foot.

REMEMBER: Forward motion = 2 beats; holding = 2 beats; returning = 2 beats. In time, progress to 4 beats each.

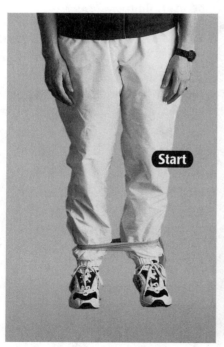 

Inner Thigh

Place normally spaced feet in loop of band. Keep one foot stationary; turn opposite foot out diagonally 45 degrees. Bring that foot forward diagonally so it crosses in front of stationary foot. Repeat with opposite foot.

REMEMBER: Forward motion = 2 beats; holding = 2 beats; returning = 2 beats. In time, progress to 4 beats each.

Diagonal Buttocks

Place normally spaced feet in loop of band. Bring one foot out diagonally to the side and back. Keep abdominals tight throughout. Repeat with opposite foot.

REMEMBER: Diagonal motion = 2 beats; holding = 2 beats; returning = 2 beats. In time, progress to 4 beats each.

Buttocks Extension

In the last exercise of the hip band series, bring one foot straight back behind its original position. Keep abdominals tight throughout. Repeat with opposite foot.

REMEMBER: Backward motion = 2 beats; holding = 2 beats; returning = 2 beats. In time, progress to 4 beats each.

Photo Shoot: Anti-Osteoporosis Workout

Stretches

Lateral Neck Stretch
Lateral Shoulder Stretch
Pectoral Stretch
Hip Flexor Stretch
Trunk Side Bend
Standing Trunk Rotation
Inner Thigh Stretch
Hamstring Stretch
    Low
    Elevated
Quadriceps Stretch
Calf Stretch
Wrist Flexor Stretch
Wrist Extensor Stretch

Starting position for standing stretches

Start all standing stretches using proper posture: ears, shoulders, hips, knees aligned; chin parallel to the ground; abdominals in, knees soft, shoulders relaxed.

Lateral Neck Stretch

While maintaining good posture (ear aligned with shoulder), bend your head sideways (ear toward shoulder). Initially, hold for 10 seconds; release and stretch more deeply for 30 seconds. Total stretch time: 40 seconds. *This stretch should be felt along the side of the neck.*

Repeat on opposite side.

Lateral Shoulder Stretch

Gently pull elbow down and toward midline of back. Initially, hold for 10 seconds; release and stretch more deeply for 30 seconds. Total stretch time: 40 seconds. *This stretch should be felt along the outside shoulder area.*

Repeat on other side.

Pectoral Stretch

Place hands palms up on your shoulders. Pull shoulder blades down and together in one motion while bringing elbows back with arms bent at elbows. *Feel a gentle stretch along the front of the shoulders.* Initially, hold for 10 seconds; release and stretch more deeply for 30 seconds. Total stretch time: 40 seconds.

Trunk Side Bend

Bend to one side. *Feel a gentle stretch along the side of the trunk.* You may put your opposite hand on your hip for stability. Initially, hold for 10 seconds; release and stretch more deeply for 30 seconds. Total stretch time: 40 seconds.

Repeat on other side.

Standing Trunk Rotation

Stand sideways to the wall, or to the back of a tall chair as pictured, approximately arms-length away. While keeping your feet stationary, turn toward the wall using your arms to gently pull into further rotation. Initially, hold for 10 seconds; release and stretch more deeply for 30 seconds. Total stretch time: 40 seconds. *This stretch should be felt in the middle part of the back.*

Repeat on opposite side.

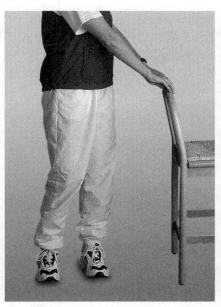 

Hip Flexor Stretch

Place one leg in front of the other, with the knee of the forward leg slightly bent. Keep your lower back straight. Tighten buttocks. Press hips forward *to feel stretch along the front of the hip.* Initially, hold for 10 seconds; release and stretch more deeply for 30 seconds. Total stretch time: 40 seconds. Repeat on other side.

Inner Thigh Stretch

Keep your back upright. Move left leg (knee bent) to the left to stretch right inner thigh. Press right leg toward ground. *Feel stretch along inside of right leg.* Repeat on the right side to stretch left inner thigh. Initially, hold for 10 seconds; release and stretch more deeply for 30 seconds. Total stretch time: 40 seconds.

Repeat on other side.

Hamstring Stretch
Low

With your back straight and weight on back leg, move one leg forward, with heel on ground. Press forward leg gently toward ground. Flex foot of the forward leg up to exaggerate the stretch. Initially, hold for 10 seconds; release and stretch more deeply for 30 seconds. Total stretch time: 40 seconds. *This stretch should be felt along the back of the thigh.*

Repeat with opposite leg

or

Elevated

Stand with your lower back straight and one foot on a stool. Then lean forward at the hip. Do not round your back. Initially, hold for 10 seconds; release and stretch more deeply for 30 seconds. Total stretch time: 40 seconds. *This stretch should be felt along the back of the thigh.*

Repeat on opposite side.

Quadriceps Stretch

Standing upright, bring your heel to your buttocks by grasping the foot with whichever is comfortable for your body. Do not lean forward at waist. Initially, hold for 10 seconds; release and stretch more deeply for 30 seconds. Total stretch time: 40 seconds. *This stretch should be felt along the front of the thigh.*

Repeat on opposite side.

Photo Shoot: Anti-Osteoporosis Workout

Calf Stretch

With your toes pointing forward, lean forward. Keep your body straight with your heels on the floor. Maintain arch in foot. Perform with knee of back leg straight. *Feel a gentle stretch in the calf.* Initially, hold for 10 seconds; release and stretch more deeply for 30 seconds. Total stretch time: 40 seconds.

Repeat on opposite side.

Wrist Flexor Stretch

Extend your arm in front of you with elbow locked (arm straight). Use the other hand to gently pull your hand and fingers up. Initially, hold for 10 seconds; release and stretch more deeply for 30 seconds. Total stretch time: 40 seconds. *This stretch should be felt along the palm side of the forearm.*

Repeat on other side.

Wrist Extensor Stretch

Extend your arm in front of you with the elbow locked (arm straight). Use the other hand to gently pull your hand and fingers down. Initially, hold for 10 seconds; release and stretch more deeply for 30 seconds. Total stretch time: 40 seconds. *This stretch should be felt along the upper side of the forearm.*

Repeat on other side.

Photo Shoot: Comprehensive Workout

Strength Training

Toe Raise
Heel Raise
Diagonal Leaning Lunge
Advanced Backward Lunge
Mini-squat with Band
One-leg Squat with Band
Trunk Side Bend
Biceps with Band
Triceps with Band
Shoulder Flexion/Extension
Upper Back Builder
Shoulder Blade Squeeze
Wall Push-up
    Hands Wide
    Hands Narrow
Wrist Flexion
Wrist Extension
Hip Series with Band
    Outer Thigh
    Quadriceps
    Inner Thigh
    Diagonal Buttocks
    Buttocks Extension

Stretches

Lateral Neck Stretch
Diagonal Neck Stretch
Shoulder Stretch
Lateral Shoulder Stretch
Overhead Shoulder Stretch
Pectoral Stretch
Trunk Side Bend
Standing Trunk Rotation
Hip Flexor Stretch
Inner Thigh Stretch
Hamstring Stretch
    Low
    Elevated
Quadriceps
Calf Stretch
    Gastrocnemius
    Soleus
Wrist Flexor Stretch
Wrist Extensor Stretch

Comprehensive Workout

The Comprehensive Workout contains all the components of the 20-minute and the Anti-osteoporosis Workouts plus supplementary stretching and strengthening exercises. This program can be performed on those days when you have more time or you can pick and choose specific exercises from this program to meet your unique fitness needs. However you use it, this program should be performed three times per week, spaced by the Mat Workout or one rest day.

Photo Shoot: Comprehensive Workout

Strength Training

Toe Raise
Heel Raise
Diagonal Leaning Lunge
Advanced Backward Lunge
Mini-squat with Band
One-leg Squat with Band
Trunk Side Bend
Biceps with Band
Triceps with Band
Shoulder Flexion/Extension
Upper Back Builder
Shoulder Blade Squeeze
Wall Push-up
    Hands Wide
    Hands Narrow
Wrist Flexion
Wrist Extension
Hip Series with Band
    Outer Thigh
    Quadriceps
    Inner Thigh
    Diagonal Buttocks
    Buttocks Extension

Toe Raise

Starting with one foot, raise toes off the floor, then slowly lower toes back to the floor. Repeat on opposite side. Progress to raising both feet simultaneously.

REMEMBER: Lifting = 2 beats; holding = 2 beats; returning = 2 beats. In time, progress to 4 beats each.

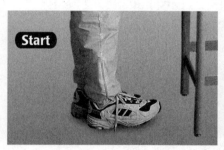

Heel Raise

Raise both heels off the floor, then slowly lower heels to the floor. Progress to one foot, placing the opposite foot behind ankle of foot to be raised. Raise the heel of the foot that is on floor. Repeat with opposite foot.

REMEMBER: Lifting = 2 beats; holding = 2 beats; returning = 2 beats. In time, progress to 4 beats each.

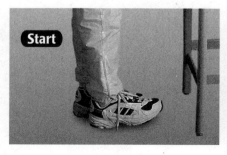

Diagonal Leaning Lunge

Bring one leg forward with that foot turned out diagonally 45 degrees. While maintaining an erect torso, bend the knee of the forward leg until the knee is over the foot. Hold 2 beats and return to starting position. Progress to advanced backward lunge.

Repeat with opposite leg.

REMEMBER: Forward motion = 2 beats; holding = 2 beats; returning = 2 beats. In time, progress to 4 beats each.

Start

Finish

Advanced Backward Lunge

Step backward, lower knee of back leg toward the floor in smooth motion keeping back straight. Keep knee of forward leg aligned with top of foot.

Repeat with opposite leg.

REMEMBER: Lowering = 2 beats; holding = 2 beats; returning = 2 beats. In time, progress to 4 beats each.

Mini-squat with Band

Stand on band and bend knees. Grasping the band in each hand, straighten slowly against resistance of band. Maintain upright posture throughout exercise. Progress to one-leg squats with band.

REMEMBER: Upward motion = 2 beats; holding = 2 beats; returning = 2 beats. In time, progress to 4 beats each.

One-leg Squat with Band

Put one foot forward with knee bent. Place band under forward foot. Grasp band keeping the low back straight; straighten knee slowly.

Repeat on opposite side.

REMEMBER: Straightening = 2 beats; holding = 2 beats; returning = 2 beats. In time, progress to 4 beats each.

Trunk Side Bend

Stand on band with one foot. Grasp band in hand. Bend in opposite direction against resistance of band. Keep back in line with hips.

Repeat on opposite side.

REMEMBER: Leaning motion = 2 beats; holding = 2 beats; returning = 2 beats. In time, progress to 4 beats each.

Biceps with Band

Stand on band and grasp ends of band, palms facing forward. Keep elbows stationary and next to your sides. Bring hands toward shoulders, bending elbows.

REMEMBER: Lifting = 2 beats; holding = 2 beats; returning = 2 beats. In time, progress to 4 beats each.

Triceps with Band

Grasp band as for biceps exercise, but with palms facing body. Bring elbows slightly behind the body and hold them stationary. Extend the forearms back, bringing hands in line with elbows.

REMEMBER: Extending = 2 beats; holding = 2 beats; returning = 2 beats. In time, progress to 4 beats each.

Shoulder Flexion/Extension

Stand on band and grasp ends of band, palms facing each other. Bring one hand forward as you bring the opposite hand back.

REMEMBER: Forward and backward motion = 2 beats; holding = 2 beats; returning = 2 beats. In time, progress to 4 beats each.

Upper Back Builder

Stand on band, and grasp ends in each hand. Point thumbs up. Raise arms to form a 45-degree angle. Stay below shoulder level.

REMEMBER: Lifting = 2 beats; holding = 2 beats; returning = 2 beats. In time, progress to 4 beats each.

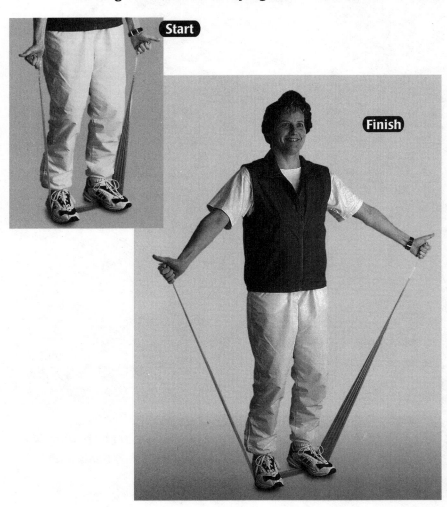

Shoulder Blade Squeeze

Bring elbows up to shoulder level. Keep elbows bent and grasp band in hands. Pull hands away from each other while pulling elbows back and squeezing shoulder blades together.

REMEMBER: Pulling = 2 beats; holding = 2 beats; returning = 2 beats. In time, progress to 4 beats each.

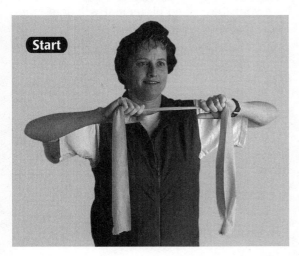

Wall Push-up

With body aligned (ears, shoulders, hips, and knees in line), perform standing push-ups against the wall. Be certain that back is not allowed to sag and head is not allowed to drop forward in front of the shoulders. Start at arms-length from the wall. Move forward smoothly toward the wall, bending elbows outward. Progress to hands on a counter top, then on the floor with body weight resting on bent knees, and then on the floor with knees straight pushing off from your toes. Hand placement will determine the muscles used.

Hands Wide

Works shoulders, chest muscles, and triceps. Place hands on wall approximately shoulder-width apart. Hands are tilted toward one another.

REMEMBER: **Forward motion = 2 beats; holding = 2 beats; returning = 2 beats. In time, progress to 4 beats each.**

Hands Narrow

Emphasizes triceps strengthening. Place hands on wall with hands in front of your face. Place your left and right hands next to one another forming a triangle with your index fingers and thumbs.

REMEMBER: **Forward motion = 2 beats; holding = 2 beats; returning = 2 beats. In time, progress to 4 beats each.**

Wrist Flexion

Hold band in one hand with palm up and hand and wrist bent down. Stand on the other end of band. Curl wrist up and to *neutral* (hand and wrist aligned with forearm). Repeat with opposite hand.

**REMEMBER: Lifting = 2 beats; holding = 2 beats;
returning = 2 beats. In time, progress to 4 beats each.**

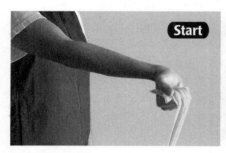 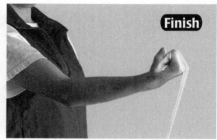

Wrist Extension

Hold band in one hand with palm down and hand and wrist aligned with forearm. Stand on the other end of the band. Bring wrist up. Repeat with opposite hand.

**REMEMBER: Lifting = 2 beats; holding = 2 beats;
returning = 2 beats. In time, progress to 4 beats each.**

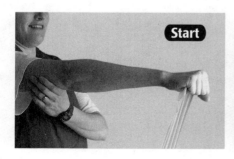 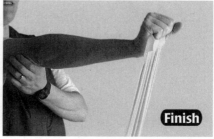

Hip Series with Band

For best results, complete this full series of five exercises one foot at a time.

Outer Thigh

Tie band into a six- to eight-inch loop and place it around your ankles. Your feet should be shoulder-width apart. Keep one foot stationary and bring opposite foot to the side. Touch foot to ground and return to starting position. Repeat with opposite foot.

REMEMBER: Side motion = 2 beats; holding = 2 beats; returning = 2 beats. In time, progress to 4 beats each.

Quadriceps

Spread feet apart until the band is taut (about shoulder width). Keep one foot stationary; bring the opposite leg forward by placing the foot directly in front of its original position. Touch the forward foot down and return to resting position. Repeat with opposite foot.

REMEMBER: Forward motion = 2 beats; holding = 2 beats; returning = 2 beats. In time, progress to 4 beats each.

Inner Thigh

Place normally spaced feet in loop of band. Keep one foot stationary; turn opposite foot out diagonally 45 degrees. Bring that foot forward diagonally so it crosses in front of stationary foot. Repeat with opposite foot.

REMEMBER: Diagonal motion = 2 beats; holding = 2 beats; returning = 2 beats. In time, progress to 4 beats each.

Diagonal Buttocks

Place normally spaced feet in loop of band. Bring one foot out diagonally to the side and back. Keep abdominals tight throughout. Repeat on opposite side.

REMEMBER: Diagonal motion = 2 beats; holding = 2 beats; returning = 2 beats. In time, progress to 4 beats each.

Buttocks Extension

In the last exercise of the hip band series, bring one foot straight back behind its original position. Keep abdominals tight throughout. Repeat with opposite foot.

REMEMBER: Backward motion = 2 beats; holding = 2 beats; returning = 2 beats. In time, progress to 4 beats each.

Photo Shoot: Comprehensive Workout

Stretches

Lateral Neck Stretch
Diagonal Neck Stretch
Shoulder Stretch
Lateral Shoulder Stretch
Overhead Shoulder Stretch
Pectoral Stretch
Trunk Side Bend
Standing Trunk Rotation
Hip Flexor Stretch
Inner Thigh Stretch
Hamstring Stretch
    Low
    Elevated
Quadriceps Stretch
Calf Stretch
    Gastrocnemius
    Soleus
Wrist Flexor Stretch
Wrist Extensor Stretch

Starting position for standing stretches

Start all standing stretches using proper posture: ears, shoulders, hips, knees aligned; chin parallel to the ground; abdominals in, knees soft, shoulders relaxed.

Lateral Neck Stretch

While maintaining good posture (ear aligned with shoulder), bend your head sideways (ear toward shoulder). Initially, hold for 10 seconds; release and stretch more deeply for 30 seconds. Total stretch time: 40 seconds. *This stretch should be felt along the side of the neck.*

Repeat on opposite side.

Diagonal Neck Stretch

While maintaining good posture, turn your head to one side, 45 degrees from center. Look down at your underarm on that side. Initially, hold for 10 seconds; release and stretch more deeply for 30 seconds. To increase stretch, gently pull your head further into stretch. Total stretch time: 40 seconds. *This stretch should be felt along one side of the back of the neck.*

Repeat on other side.

Shoulder Stretch

Gently bring elbow across body at shoulder level. Initially, hold for 10 seconds; release and stretch more deeply for 30 seconds. Total stretch time: 40 seconds. *This stretch should be felt along the back of the shoulder.*

Repeat on other side.

Lateral Shoulder Stretch

Gently pull elbow down and toward midline of back. Initially, hold for 10 seconds; release and stretch more deeply for 30 seconds. Total stretch time: 40 seconds. *This stretch should be felt along the outside shoulder.*

Repeat on other side.

Overhead Shoulder Stretch

Interlace your fingers above your head. With palms facing upward, push arms up and slightly back. Initially, hold for 10 seconds; release and stretch more deeply for 30 seconds. Total stretch time: 40 seconds. *This stretch should be felt along the outside of the upper arm and shoulder.*

Pectoral Stretch

Place hands palms up on your shoulders. Pull shoulder blades down and together in one motion while bringing elbows back with arms bent at elbows. *Feel a gentle stretch along the front of the shoulders.* Initially, hold for 10 seconds; release and stretch more deeply for 30 seconds. Total stretch time: 40 seconds.

Trunk Side Bend

Bend to one side. *Feel a gentle stretch along the side of the trunk.* You may put your opposite hand on your hip for stability. Initially, hold for 10 seconds; release and stretch more deeply for 30 seconds. Total stretch time: 40 seconds.

Repeat on opposite side.

 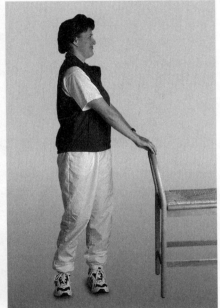

Standing Trunk Rotation

Stand sideways to the wall, or to a tall chair as pictured, approximately arms-length away. While keeping your feet stationary, turn toward the wall using your arms to gently pull into further rotation. Initially, hold for 10 seconds; release and stretch more deeply for 30 seconds. Total stretch time: 40 seconds. *This stretch should be felt in the middle part of the back.*

Repeat on opposite side.

Hip Flexor Stretch

Place one leg in front of the other, with the knee of the forward leg slightly bent. Keep your lower back straight. Tighten buttocks. Press hips forward. *Feel stretch along the front of the hip.* Initially, hold for 10 seconds; release and stretch more deeply for 30 seconds. Total stretch time: 40 seconds.

Repeat on other side.

Inner Thigh Stretch

Keep your back upright. Move left leg (knee bent) to the left to stretch right inner thigh. Press right leg toward ground. *Feel stretch along inside of right leg.* Repeat on the right side to stretch left inner thigh. Initially, hold for 10 seconds; release and stretch more deeply for 30 seconds. Total stretch time: 40 seconds.

Repeat on other side.

Hamstring Stretch
Low

With your back straight and weight on back leg, move one leg forward with heel on ground. Press forward leg gently toward ground. Flex foot of the forward leg up to exaggerate the stretch. Initially, hold for 10 seconds; release and stretch more deeply for 30 seconds. Total stretch time: 40 seconds. *This stretch should be felt along the back of the thigh.*

Repeat with opposite leg.

or

Elevated

Stand with your lower back straight and one foot on a stool. Then lean forward at the hip. Do not round your back. Initially, hold for 10 seconds; release and stretch more deeply for 30 seconds. Total stretch time: 40 seconds. *This stretch should be felt along the back of the thigh.*

Repeat on opposite side.

Quadriceps Stretch

Standing upright, bring your heel to your buttocks by grasping the foot with whichever is comfortable for your body. Do not lean forward at waist. Initially, hold for 10 seconds; release and stretch more deeply for 30 seconds. Total stretch time: 40 seconds. *This stretch should be felt along the front of the thigh.*

Repeat on opposite side.

Calf Stretch
Gastrocnemius

With your toes pointing forward, lean forward. Keep your body straight with your heels on the floor. Maintain arch in foot. Perform with knee of back leg straight. *Feel a gentle stretch in the calf.* Initially, hold for 10 seconds; release and stretch more deeply for 30 seconds. Total stretch time: 40 seconds.

Repeat on opposite side.

Soleus

With your toes pointing forward, lean forward. Keep your body straight with your heels on the floor. Maintain arch in foot. Bend knee of back leg. *Feel a gentle stretch in the calf.* Initially, hold for 10 seconds; release and stretch more deeply for 30 seconds. Total stretch time: 40 seconds.

Repeat on opposite side.

Wrist Flexor Stretch

Extend your arm in front of you with elbow locked (arm straight). Use the other hand to gently pull your hand and fingers up. Initially, hold for 10 seconds; release and stretch more deeply for 30 seconds. Total stretch time: 40 seconds. *This stretch should be felt along the palm side of the forearm.*

Repeat on opposite side.

Wrist Extensor Stretch

Extend your arm in front of you with the elbow locked (arm straight). Use the other hand to gently pull your hand and fingers down. Initially, hold for 10 seconds; release and stretch more deeply for 30 seconds. Total stretch time: 40 seconds. *This stretch should be felt along the upper side of the forearm.*

Repeat on opposite side.

And... Most Importantly, Have Fun!

Appendix

Fitness Walking Record

Record the time or miles you are in your target zone each day. Work up gradually—increase your time or miles at a rate of approximately 10 percent per week. Be sure to include two *rest* days per week in your program. (A rest day could be walking at a pace below your target zone or engaging in any form of low- to moderate- intensity activity.)

FITNESS WALKING, INC.®

	Goal	Sunday	Monday	Tuesday	Wednesday	Thursday	Friday	Saturday	Total
Week #1									
Week #2									
Week #3									
Week #4									
Week #5									
Week #6									
Week #7									
Week #8									
Week #9									
Week #10									

FITNESS WALKING, INC.®

Shape*Walking* Resistance–Strength Training Progression Chart

Begin with the color resistance band that you have determined for your starting level. Do the exercises you have chosen for 10 repetitions (reps). When you can do 10 reps easily, increase to 12 reps. When 12 reps can be done easily, increase to 15 reps. Once you can do 15 reps easily, move to the next resistance band color and start at 10 reps again. Follow this progression for each exercise. Photocopy this chart for your personal record keeping. **Always warm up before performing exercises.** Always perform exercises with good form.

NOTE: If at any time you feel pain while performing a particular exercise, STOP doing that exercise.

Date:						
Exercise	**Color/Reps**	**Color/Reps**	**Color/Reps**	**Color/Reps**	**Color/Reps**	**Color/Reps**

Resources for Walkers

Join Others Who Enjoy Walking in Minnesota...

Structured Programs

Heel to Toe Fitness Walking
Marilyn L. Bach, Ph.D.
P. O. Box 4143
Saint Paul, Minnesota 55104-0143
Fax: (651) 290-2803
E-mail: www.heeltotoe.com

WalkSport America
Sara Donovan
P. O. Box 16325
Saint Paul, Minnesota 55116
(651) 291-7138

Club Racewalk
Gary Westlund
Minneapolis. Minnesota
(612) 487-1569

Twin City Volksmarchers
Doug Wood
Minneapolis, Minnesota
(612) 929-4891

Twin City Walkers
Bob Stum
Minneapolis, Minnesota
(612) 487-1569

Walking Workshop
Sage Cowles
Sweatshop Fitness Training Center
167 Snelling Avenue North
Saint Paul, Minnesota 55104
(651) 646-8418

Activities

Minneapolis Parks & Recreation Board
310 Fourth Avenue South
Minneapolis, Minnesota 55415
(612) 661-4800

Melpomene Institute
1010 University Ave.
Saint Paul, Minnesota 55104
(651) 642-1951

Nationally

Walking Tours, Inc.
P.O. Box 84475
Vancouver, Washington 98684-0475
800-779-0353

American Volkssport Association
1001 Pat Booker Road, Suite 101
Universal City, Texas 78148-4147
(210) 659-2112
Volkssport Events: 800-830-WALK

Walking Spas

Cal-A-Vie
Vista, California
(619) 945-2055

Miraval Life in Balance Spa
Catalina, Arizona
800-825-4000

Canyon Ranch
Tucson, Arizona
and Lenox, Massachusetts
800-726-9900

Mountain Trek Fitness Retreat
Ainsworth Hot Springs, British
Columbia, Canada
800-661-5161

Golden Door
San Marcos, California
800-424-0777

New Life Hiking Spa
Killington, Vermont
800-228-4676

Green Valley Spa
Saint George, Utah
800-237-1068

Rancho La Puerta
Baja California, Mexico
800-443-7565

Lake Austin Spa Resort
Austin, Texas
800-847-5637

Selected Bibliography

Anderson, Robert A. and Jean E. Anderson. *Stretching.* Bolinas, CA: Shelter Publications, Inc., 1980. ISBN 0-936070-01-3 ISBN (Random House) 0-394-73874-8.

Bricklin, Mark and Susan G. Berg. *The Best of Prevention.* Emmaus, PA: Rodale Press, 1997. ISBN 0-87596-419-2.

"Calories Go, Fast or Slow." *Walker's World.* 1997: 5.

Clark, Nancy, M.S., R.D. "Fluids, Dehydration and Thirst Quenchers." Brookline, MA: Sports Medicine Brookline. 02167.

Cook, Brian B. and Gordon W. Stewart. *Strength Basics.* Champaign, IL: Human Kinetics, 1996.

Cowles, Sage. Fitness Walking Workshop. *Reebok Bodywalk.* Saint Paul, MN: Sweatshop, 1996.

Department of Health and Human Services. A Report of the Surgeon General. *Physical Activity and Health.* Pittsburgh, PA, 1996. ISBN 017-023-00196-5.

Gerber, Niklaus J. and Bernhard Rey. "Can Exercise Prevent Osteoporosis or Reverse Bone Loss? A Review of Controlled Longitudinal Trials." *Physiotherapy: Controlled Trials and Facts.* 14 (1991): 47–60.

Grant, Roberta. "Walk Off Weight This Winter." *Fitness.* Jan.-Feb. 1997: 40–44.

Green, Bob and Oprah Winfrey. *Make the Connection: Ten Steps to a Better Body—and a Better Life.* New York: Hyperion, 1996. ISBN 0-7868-6256-4.

Gutin, B. and M.J. Kasper. "Can Vigorous Exercise Play a Role in Osteoporosis Prevention? A Review." *Osteoporosis International.* 2 (1992): 55–69.

Heinonen, A.; P. Oja; P. Kannus; H. Sievanen; H. Haapasalo; A. Manttari; and I. Vuori. "Bone Mineral Density in Female Athletes Representing Sports with Different Loading Characteristics of the Skeleton." *Bone.* 17.3 (1995): 197–203.

Home Study Program for Senior Fitness. Sherman Oaks, CA: Aerobics and Fitness Association of America, 1991.

Hurley, Ben, Ph.D. "Strength Training in the Elderly to Enhance Health Status." *Medicine, Exercise, Nutrition, and Health.* 4 (1995): 217–29.

Iknoian, Therese. *Fitness Walking.* Champaign, IL: Human Kinetics Publishers, 1995. ISBN 0-87322-553-8.

Itjelm, Rick, P.T. "Brrr...Exercising Outdoors in Winter." *Sideline View.* Minneapolis, MN: The Institute of Athletic Medicine at Fairview Hospital. 5 December 1988: 10.

Kannus, P.; H. Sievanen; and I. Vuori. "Physical Loading, Exercise, and Bone." *Bone.* 18.1 (1996)[Suppl.]: S1–S3.

Meyers, Casey. *Walking: A Complete Guide to the Complete Exercise.* New York: Random House, 1992. ISBN 0-679-73777-4.

Otis, Carol L., M.S. with Linda Lynch. "How to Keep Your Bones Healthy." *The Physician and Sportsmedicine.* 22.1 (1994): 71–72.

Oyster, Nancy, Max Morton, and Sheri Linnell. "Physical Activity and Osteoporosis in Post-menopausal Women." *Medicine and Science in Sports and Exercise.* 16.1 (1984): 44-50.

Simkin, Ariel; Judith Ayalon; and Isaac Leichter. "Increased Trabecular Bone Density Due to Bone-Loading Exercises in Post-menopausal Osteoporotic Women." *Calcified Tissue International.* 40 (1987): 59–63.

Sinaki, Mehrsheed, M.D. and Kenneth P. Offord, M.S. "Physical Activity in Post-menopausal Women: Effect on Back Muscle Strength and Bone Mineral Density of the Spine." *Archives of Physical Medicine and Rehabilitation.* 69 (1988): 277–80.

Smith, Everett L.; Catherine Gilligan; Marianne McAdam; Cynthia P. Ensign; and Patricia E. Smith. "Deterring Bone Loss by Exercise Intervention in Premenopausal and Postmenopausal Women." *Calcified Tissue International.* 44 (1989): 312–21.

Smith, Everett L. and Catherine Gilligan. "Physical Activity Effects on Bone Metabolism." *Calcified Tissue International.* 49 (1991)[Suppl]: S50–S54.

Westcott, Wayne L. "Muscular Strength and Endurance." *Personal Trainer Manual: The Resource for Fitness Instructors.* Ed. Mitchell Sudy. Boston: Reebok University Press, 1996. 235–74. ISBN   0-9618161-2-0.

Yanker, Gary and Kathy Burton. *Walking Medicine.* New York: McGraw-Hill, 1993. ISBN 0-7-072265-X [PB].

Notes

Notes

Notes